# OPENING DOORS
# to
# QUALITY WRITING

## Ideas for writing inspired by great writers for ages 6 to 9

## BOB COX

C000163607

First published by

Crown House Publishing Ltd
Crown Buildings, Bancyfelin, Carmarthen, Wales, SA33 5ND, UK
www.crownhouse.co.uk

and

Crown House Publishing Company LLC
PO Box 2223, Williston, VT 05495
www.crownhousepublishing.com

First published 2016. Reprinted 2017.

British Library Cataloguing-in-Publication Data
A catalogue entry for this book is available
from the British Library.

Print ISBN 978-178583013-6
Mobi ISBN 978-178583122-5
ePub ISBN 978-178583123-2
ePDF ISBN 978-178583124-9

LCCN 2015953351

Printed and bound in the UK by
Gomer Press, Llandysul, Ceredigion

For Vicky, with love

# Contents

# Acknowledgements

I have been able to develop 'Opening Doors' into a series of books thanks to the feedback and encouragement from schools across the UK, and their trialling of materials. It is much appreciated and, indeed, inspiring to hear from so many schools who are using the ideas.

In particular, I would like to thank staff and pupils from:

St Augustine's Catholic Primary School, Frimley, Surrey

Balcarrass School and associated teaching alliance schools, Cheltenham, Gloucestershire

Boxgrove Primary School and teaching alliance schools, Guildford, Surrey

Broadstone First School, Poole, Dorset

Church Crookham Junior School, Fleet, Hampshire

Churchfields Junior School, South Woodford, Redbridge

Crofton Hammond Infants School, Hampshire

Epsom Partnership, Surrey

Fort Hill Community School, Basingstoke, Hampshire

Frogmore Junior School, Hampshire

Furze Platt Infants School, Maidenhead, RBWM

Furze Platt Secondary School, Maidenhead, RBWM

Hawley Primary School, Hampshire

Hook Junior School, Hampshire

Netley Abbey Primary School, Hampshire

Portsmouth Grammar School, Hampshire

Ravenscote Junior School, Camberley, Surrey

Ringwood National Teaching School, Hampshire

Robin Hood Junior School, Sutton, Surrey

Roch Community Primary School, Pembrokeshire

Saturday Challenge Enrichment Centre, Fleet, Hampshire

St Francis RC Primary School, Maidenhead, RBWM

St Teresa's Catholic Primary School, Wokingham, Berkshire

The Grange Community Junior School, Farnborough, Hampshire

Wandsworth Local Authority

Westfields Junior School, Yateley, Hampshire

Wicor Primary School, Fareham, Hampshire

Teachers and schools in Poole and across Dorset, Surrey and Wandsworth

Also:

Potential Plus UK

Osiris Educational

And especially:

Crown House Publishing for their continued amazing support and enthusiasm.

A word is dead
When it is said,
Some say.
I say it just
Begins to live
That day.

**Emily Dickinson**

# Introduction

*Opening Doors to Quality Writing* is a companion book to *Opening Doors to Famous Poetry and Prose* (2014). There are two books, one for ages 6 to 9 and one for ages 10 to 13. The idea is that teachers will be supported, in flexible and creative ways, to use quality literary texts to stimulate quality writing. My theme has continued to be the exploration of poetry and prose from long ago, sometimes termed 'literary heritage' texts. My aim is to suggest ways in which the evident quality of the writing can be exploited by schools to develop exciting journeys in reading, writing, speaking and listening for their pupils. I am seeing many teachers successfully use the scope and depth which literature can offer to inspire high standards, mastery learning and, above all, a love of language in its many forms. My criteria for choosing the texts has been that they support the need for greater knowledge of literature from the past and provide the scope needed for deeper learning in English.

All the units should help you to make links from understanding the challenging texts to maximising the huge potential for quality writing. I hope your pupils will enjoy the writing ideas suggested and that you and your pupils will be inspired to devise your own! You should find the level of expectation goes up and, with it, the children's writing should become more quirky, creative and unusual – after all, it's great writers who have inspired the class! In this book, I have been able to include examples of remarkable pupils' work, of all abilities, and I have included a story of my own. I am always encouraging teachers to write with their pupils, so it's a way of showing that it can be a natural thing to do. Writing creatively maintains my own awareness of how difficult, yet fulfilling, it can be and, since we are encouraging quality writing, we can all be partners in the process.

In my extensive travels as a teacher and an educational consultant, I have often found that progress is limited either by a model which becomes too much of a straightjacket or by an unwillingness to adapt the model to suit particular classes or pupils. Feedback from *Opening Doors to Famous Poetry and Prose* has frequently emphasised the confidence which can develop when creative ideas are used as a starting point, – for example:

> Thank you for reigniting our love of quality texts and giving us fantastic planning and teaching ideas to encourage all abilities to access the texts.
>
> ### *Churchfields Junior School Conference, 2015*

Support and enthusiasm from teachers is essential. It is the teachers who will take ideas deeper, invent new questions and present their lessons in new planning shapes. The books (and the conferences I run) are designed to signpost ways to access a harder curriculum so that confidence and self-evaluation can grow. When challenging texts become the norm in classroom practice, there are significant implications for methodology and resourcing, so the 'Opening Doors' series is a complement to approaches being trialled in schools which involve all learners working on the same content and with the same objectives.

Overwhelmingly, however, teachers have been asking for more of the quality texts themselves and more ways in which all abilities can access them. So, here are fifteen units of work which should help to stimulate many innovative ways for all your pupils to enjoy literature and write with originality. Schools working with the 'Opening Doors' strategies have tended to report:

❦ More teacher empowerment and confidence.

❦ More knowledge building for pupils and teachers.

❦ A growing confidence with literature, including poetry.

❦ A tendency to move to using 'English' as the subject name rather than 'literacy'.

❦ Planning from the top becoming a norm.

❦ Planning for mastery learning becoming a norm.

❦ Improved comprehension skills.

❦ Improved quality writing and associated excitement.

'Opening Doors' is intended to add a more challenging dimension to English teaching, but all learners can find that doors have been opened because access is always emphasised. The diagram on page 4 provides a framework for the many ways in which quality writing can be achieved.

The pattern you will find across the units marks out the major principles which can support a richer diet in English:

❦ Texts with scope for creativity and curiosity.

❦ The need for a range of access strategies.

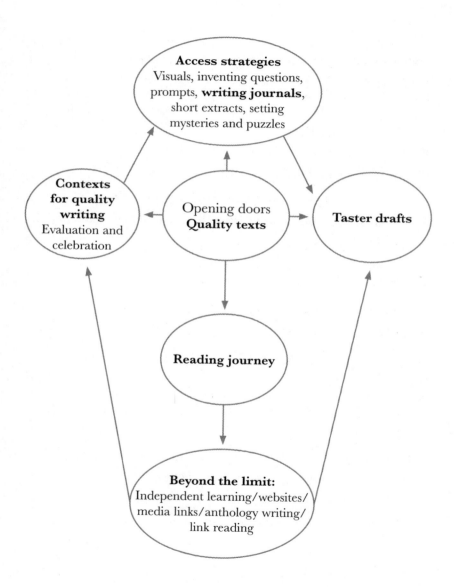

❦ The recommendation to write early on in the process via **taster drafts**.

❦ Using a range of assessment for learning strategies and 'excellent responses' criteria.

❦ Emphasising the wonder of the text revealed.

❦ Offering harder, evaluative questions sooner.

❦ Linking the learning about quality texts with the application required for quality writing.

❦ Including 'beyond the limit' reading and writing ideas at appropriate points.

❦ Planning lessons in shapes which suit the objectives.

Both the diagram and the questions across the units are set out in a radial way with choices, options and routes critical to differentiation methods which can be planned according to progress. At all times, great writers and great writing lead the way so the inspiration comes from them, with pupils guided by the immense talent of their teachers. There is no need to be limited by any single pedagogy. Approaches can be constantly evaluated and altered according to outcomes. I love the feedback I get from teachers telling me they have linked the text with a more modern one, negotiated fresh questions or converted the task into a different medium.

At the heart of the 'Opening Doors' concept is the need for the teachers to use literary texts as starting points for their own invention. That mindset is bound to spread to the pupils. They will be suggesting approaches too – and why not?

Part 1

# Opening doors
# to poetry

# His Waistcoat and Trousers Were Made of Pork Chops

## 'The New Vestments' by Edward Lear

How well can you understand and write 'clever nonsense'?

### Access strategies

What better access strategy could there be than to study an illustration first and start creating words and ideas immediately!

Try a **question maze**. The pupils have to ask as many questions as possible which have been raised by the picture. Just ask them what puzzles them about the picture. If they need starter prompts try these:

❦ What is on his head?

❦ Which colours would you use for different parts of the clothing?

❦ What is unexpected?

You may find it useful to magnify the picture if you can or crop sections of it for discussion.

Write harder conceptual questions (you could call them **killer questions**) on sticky notes and place these in the middle of each table.

Your pupils should write their attempted answers on different coloured sticky notes and place these around the question. Now turn the 'answers' over so no one can see them and ask the groups to change tables and try answering another group's questions. Compare the answers from the different groups later.

When you feed back on this in a **mini-plenary**, you can begin the process of guiding pupils towards the idea of 'clever nonsense'. Content which is, at first reading, absurd, can be very clever indeed or it can seem just ridiculous.

The following points might emerge:

❦ The images are surprising and unlikely but there is a kind of pattern too.

❦ The images could be unpleasant or just fun.

❦ The **rhyming couplets** and regular rhythm support the jolly, whimsical feel.

At any appropriate point, offer the beginning of Edward Lear's poem, 'The New Vestments', which might support your teaching strategies and your pupils' engagement:

---

There lived an old man in the Kingdom of Tess,

Who invented a purely original dress;

And when it was perfectly made and complete,

He opened the door, and walked into the street.

---

I love reaching this point where children wait in anticipation for more! That's because they have been engaged with learning about images, so they are ready to move on.

Here are the first two **stanzas**:

Source 3

### The New Vestments

There lived an old man in the Kingdom of Tess,
Who invented a purely original dress;
And when it was perfectly made and complete,
He opened the door, and walked into the street.

By way of a hat, he'd a loaf of Brown Bread,
In the middle of which he inserted his head; −
His Shirt was made up of no end of dead Mice,
The warmth of whose skins was quite fluffy and nice; −
His Drawers were of Rabbit-skins; − so were his Shoes; −
His Stockings were skins, − but it is not known whose; −
His Waistcoat and Trowsers were made of Pork Chops; −
His Buttons were Jujubes, and Chocolate Drops; −
His Coat was all Pancakes with Jam for a border,
And a girdle of Biscuits to keep it in order;
And he wore over all, as a screen from bad weather,
A Cloak of green Cabbage-leaves stitched all together.

A rapid **taster draft** should now produce some inspired writing. Why not ask the children to use some of the clothes but invent different images for a different old man or woman from the Kingdom of Tess?

| Item | New image |
|---|---|
| Waistcoat | Corn on the cob |
| Hat | |
| Cloak | |

The pupils should then write just one stanza which brings their new character to life!

# Reading journeys

If your pupils can identify and understand more about the subtlety of Lear's methods, then they can apply this thinking in their own writing. Try using an open question which encourages synthesis and question making. You can intervene with the support strategies as appropriate.

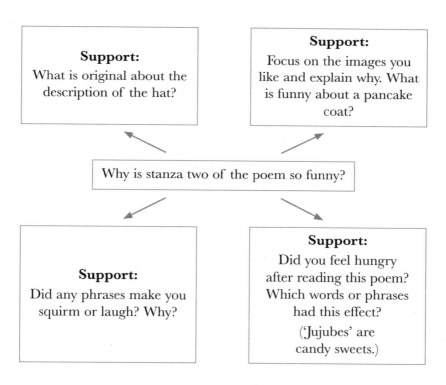

**Support:**
What is original about the description of the hat?

**Support:**
Focus on the images you like and explain why. What is funny about a pancake coat?

Why is stanza two of the poem so funny?

**Support:**
Did any phrases make you squirm or laugh? Why?

**Support:**
Did you feel hungry after reading this poem? Which words or phrases had this effect?
('Jujubes' are candy sweets.)

The resulting feedback should **dig deeper** into a possible definition of 'nonsense'. As the links are made between the quality of the text and the children's writing potential, an 'excellent responses will' list may start to emerge which can help the writing process.

**Excellent responses will:**

❦ Craft unusual images – funny but not silly!

- ❧ Use punctuation flexibly to emphasise meaning and support recitation (e.g. the dashes Lear utilises).

- ❧ Use **rhyming couplets** for flow and humour as an option.

- ❧ Use striking visual pictures in words.

- ❧ Create a pattern for the 'nonsense'.

- ❧ Be original!

Now, ask the children to apply this thinking to the 'beyond the limit' titles below.

# Beyond the limit

**Link reading** can include the wealth of 'nonsense' there is to read:

- ❧ 'The New Vestments' (the complete poem) by Edward Lear

- ❧ 'The Owl and the Pussycat' by Edward Lear

- ❧ 'Colonel Fazackerley Butterworth-Toast' by Charles Causley

- ❧ 'Mr Pennycomequick' by Charles Causley

- ❧ *My First Book of Nonsense Poems* edited by John Foster

Link with:

- ❧ 'The Hippocrump' by James Reeves (Unit 2).

- ❧ *Uncle David's Nonsensical Story about Giants and Fairies* by Catherine Sinclair (Unit 11).

- ❧ The *Alice's Adventures in Wonderland* Unit (Unit 11 in *Opening Doors to Famous Poetry and Prose*).

Other poets who sometimes write 'nonsense':

- ❦ John Agard
- ❦ Hilaire Belloc
- ❦ Spike Milligan
- ❦ Ogden Nash
- ❦ Jack Prelutsky
- ❦ Michael Rosen

For deeper extension for the more able, Giuseppe Arcimboldo's painting *Fruit Basket* (which you can easily find online) may provide some inspiration to write about a face which is made up of fruit or some other kind of food.

Sir Edward Strachey, a nineteenth century writer, said, 'Nonsense … has shown itself to be a true work of the imagination, a child of genius.' High praise indeed – and he mentions Edward Lear as the person who gave nonsense its 'due place and honour'.

Your most able pupils should be able to read many poems by Lear and produce an anthology of their own nonsense poems, short and long. Lear's poems are available online at: http://www.poemhunter.com/edward-lear.

# Wings to fly

Titles will abound to link with the learning depth afforded by 'The New Vestments', but try to differentiate the learning to suit the individual. You might consider reading more of the poem first and then offer a variety of tasks and opportunities around the classroom. Keep tracking the quality text to a quality writing journey!

One writing task could be to continue the poem to see what reception the old man gets in the Kingdom of Tess. Some pupils might need stanza three first:

He had walked a short way, when he heard a great noise,
Of all sorts of Beasticles, Birdlings, and Boys;–
And from every long street and dark lane in the town
Beasts, Birdles, and Boys in a tumult rushed down.
Two Cows and a half ate his Cabbage-leaf Cloak;–
Four Apes seized his Girdle, which vanished like smoke;–
Three Kids ate up half of his Pancaky Coat,–
And the tails were devour'd by an ancient He Goat;–

Some children may be ready for the full poem which is hilarious (see http://www.poemhunter.com/poem/the-new-vestments/)! You will know how to handle the old man's drawers coming off and his naked flight at the end!

Other Lear poems which would work well alongside 'The New Vestments' include 'The Jumblies' and 'Calico Pie'.

Planning nonsense poetry should be great fun. Don't keep to the conventional – it doesn't fit the theme! I would expect to see a huge range of methods – for example, visual maps meandering over sugar paper, drafts crossing interactive whiteboards and image making on tablets or laptops. The challenge with nonsense poetry is coherence, which returns us to our main theme: nonsense is also clever!

### Bob says ...

*There is a huge opportunity here for risk-taking! Yes, a few young writers might get carried away with dead mice and invent something truly awful. We just have to tell them if their images become a bit daft. Some of your pupils will pick up the need for coherence within the nonsense and write something very special!*

It certainly should be 'wings to fly, not drills to kill', with this choice of titles and ideas:

- ❦ Continue the poem about what happens to the old man when he goes out.
- ❦ Instead of a man with 'original dress', write a nonsense poem about a man, woman, boy or girl with an 'original house'.
- ❦ Keep the same old man in your poem but change the hat, the buttons and the cloak!
- ❦ Your old man or woman journeys to a new kingdom and gets a different reception! How is this different?

❦ Write a nonsense poem for today, inventing a character who journeys through your own town, city or village.

❦ Take the pork chop image and use it in any way in your own nonsense poem!

Here are some possibilities if any pupils are stuck and need additional support:

❦ Take a line you like, for example: 'His Coat was all Pancakes with Jam for a border'. Focus on this image and write six more lines about the way the pancakes and jam look and feel.

❦ Take the line: 'And a girdle of Biscuits to keep it in order'. Invent a new girdle to go round the old man and write six lines describing it – but it must not be biscuits!

# Prefabulous Animiles

## 'The Hippocrump' by James Reeves

Your challenge is to create an amazing 'prefabulous animile'! How well can you do it?

## Access strategies

You will find James Reeves's poetry books, *Prefabulous Animiles* (1957) and *More Prefabulous Animiles* (1975), a source of huge invention, creativity, originality and fun! 'The Hippocrump' is a particularly fascinating poem and the illustration provided on page 20 is a good starting point for your questioning:

❦ Can you give the creature a name?

❦ What might its habitat be?

❦ Is it a frightening or funny poem?

Different groups could now be given the task of describing particular parts of the Hippocrump. The following list might help:

❦ Body

❦ Skin or hide

❦ Teeth

- ❦ Humps
- ❦ Hair
- ❦ Beard
- ❦ Neck

This encourages deeper thinking in terms of detail and will support sustained writing later on. Bring the different parts together in a large group for a **word mosaic**. You now have a class version of the Hippocrump, and a bold reading of the first **stanza** can follow:

Source 6

Along the valley of the Ump
Gallops the fearful Hippocrump.
His hide is leathery and thick;
His eyelids open with a *Click!*
His mouth he closes with a *Clack!*
He has three humps upon his back;
On each of these there grows a score
Of horny spikes, and sometimes more.
His hair is curly, thick and brown;
Beneath his chin a beard hangs down.
He has eight feet with hideous claws;
His neck is long – and O his jaws!
The boldest falters in his track
To hear those hundred teeth go *Clack!*
The Hippocrump is fierce indeed,

But if he eats the baneful weed

That grows beside the Purple Lake,

His hundred teeth begin to ache.

---

Exploit all the fun by moving quickly into a **taster draft** with these writing opportunities:

❦ Develop the setting – the valley of the Ump and the Purple Lake.

❦ Develop the movement of the Hippocrump – what happens?

❦ Develop the importance of the baneful (harmful) weed.

Work in groups using a **plus, minus, interesting** (PMI) chart to sift and sort which are the best ideas before choosing one for the **mini-plenary** feedback session. Here is an example.

| Plus | Minus | Interesting |
|------|-------|-------------|
| Hippocrump takes fruit from a tree using his long neck. | Is there enough action? | We could link this with an episode taking the fruit to the lake. |
| Could be funny. | | Is there another animile in the lake? |

Sift through the ideas and identify those showing the most coherence and originality. Return to these in the 'wings to fly' section.

Robyn Welsh (Year 1) from Broadstone First School in Poole had the added help of exploring both 'The Hippocrump' and 'The Catipoce' from *Prefabulous Animiles*. Her 'My Tiny Dragon' shows that even 5-year-olds can be inspired by a poet like Reeves – and a great teacher!

### My Tiny Dragon

Once upon a time there was a little dragon in a tree. One day he went for a walk. Suddenly, he tripped over a little rock. Luckily he didn't die; instead he made a friend – the dinosaur. The end.

Isabel (Year 1) from the same school took a different approach, with help from the 'Three Billy Goats Gruff' story:

### The Troll

Once upon a time there was a sticky, horrid troll. Not many people knew this but he is made of marshmallow and chocolate.

Isabel's teacher had written, 'I love that. Horrid on the outside and yummy on the inside.' Now, that's inspiring marking!

*Bob says ...*

*Just when I think I understand something about children's potential, I am proved wrong again. I wrote this book for ages 6 to 9 and yet I have been receiving work like Robyn's and Isabel's from Year 1 classrooms. Maybe we would be better off abandoning targets and expectations and simply inviting all our pupils to surprise us – they probably will!*

# Reading journeys

Planning from the top is a necessary habit to ensure all learners are included in ambitious learning journeys. Use an open question to challenge your pupils but also consider the support statements for those who get stuck. The radial layout should help you to make personalised decisions on behalf of your pupils. It makes differentiation a natural process and can be adapted according to need and progress.

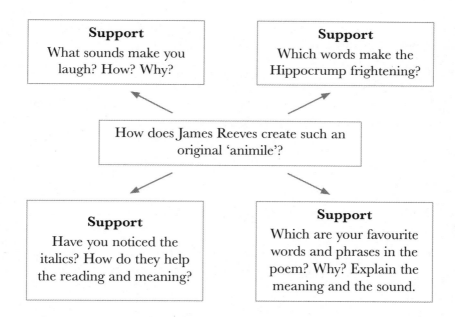

**Support**
What sounds make you laugh? How? Why?

**Support**
Which words make the Hippocrump frightening?

How does James Reeves create such an original 'animile'?

**Support**
Have you noticed the italics? How do they help the reading and meaning?

**Support**
Which are your favourite words and phrases in the poem? Why? Explain the meaning and the sound.

Apart from asking for written answers to the above, many other approaches are possible:

🐌 Different groups could explore different sections and feed back their answers.

🐌 Each group could deepen expertise on a particular section. Experts could then **jigsaw** with other groups to talk about ideas around the table in timed sessions.

🐌 Spelling is explored in context – for example, find other 'ie' words (like 'fierce') or 'eous' words (like 'hideous').

Remember, whole-class discussions can support **new learning** and selected teaching points.

The success criteria below is designed to help you gauge how technical you want to be. There is a lot to be learnt from James Reeves, so try to show how specific aspects of the poetry you are teaching will help your budding writers to be budding poets.

**Excellent responses will**:

- ❧ Show how punctuation contributes to meaning – for example, the dash after 'long'.

- ❧ Show how the **iambic metre** supports the dramatic movement of the Hippocrump.

- ❧ Show how the **assonance** litters the **stanza** with rhyming vowels, giving movement to the emerging description of the Hippocrump.

- ❧ Mention the italics and the effect the reading should have as the **onomatopoeia** rings around the room.

- ❧ Explore the way simple words link together for a young reader to build an impression of both danger and fun – the 'horny spikes' sound threatening but the 'beard' is hilarious.

*Bob says ...*

*The 'excellent responses will' lists in this book are designed to support deeper learning, so the children are experiencing poetry and having fun but they are also learning **about** poetry. I work with schools to use the lists for teacher continuing professional development (CPD). Just* *choose which aspects of this list are priorities for your class and for each pupil. The more knowledgeable you become, the more progress your pupils will make towards a level of mastery. The text provides the inspiration!*

You will also want to read the whole poem and extend the **reading journey**. This is where deeper knowledge and better learning combine so the children can appreciate the overall effect. Have fun by starting again with the first stanza and then adding the next three:

---

**Source 7**

### The Hippocrump

Then how the creature stamps and roars
Along the Ump's resounding shores!
The drowsy cattle faint with fright;
The birds fall flat, the fish turn white.
Even the rocks begin to shake;
The children in their beds awake;
The old ones quiver, quail, and quake.
'Alas!' they cry. 'Make no mistake,
It is *Himself* – he's got the Ache
From eating by the Purple Lake!'
Some say, 'It is *Old You-know-who* –
He's in a rage: what *shall* we do?'
'Lock up the barns, protect the stores,
Bring all the pigs and sheep indoors!'

They call upon their god, Agw-ump
To save them from the Hippocrump.
'What's that I hear go hop-skip-jump?
He's coming! Stand aside there!' *Bump!*
*Lump-lump!* – 'He's on the bridge now!' – *Lump!*
'I hear his tail' – *ker-flump, ker-flump!*
'I see the prickles on his hump!
It *is*, it IS – the Hippocrump!
Defend us now, O Great Agw-ump!'

Thus prayed the dwellers by the Ump.
Their prayer was heard. A broken stump
Caught the intruder in the rump.
He slipped into the foaming river,
Whose icy water quenched his fever,
Then while the creature floundering lay,
The timid people ran away;
And when the morrow dawned serene
The Hippocrump was no more seen.
Glad hymns of joy the people raised:
'For ever Great Agw-ump be praised!'

# Beyond the limit

At any appropriate point in this unit, do flood your pupils with other 'Prefabulous Animiles'. The collections are available to order from your library, from bookstores or on the internet. Reading out the names of some of my favourites will whet the appetite:

- The Snitterjipe
- The Doze
- The Osc
- The Troke
- The Bogus-Boo

Other collections that may help your pupils' enjoyment would be:

- 'Jabberwocky' from *Alice's Adventures in Wonderland* by Lewis Carroll (see Unit 11 of *Opening Doors to Famous Poetry and Prose*)
- *Flanimals* by Ricky Gervais
- *Meet My Folks* by Ted Hughes
- *The Hobbit* and *The Lord of the Rings* by J. R. R. Tolkien

In *Meet My Folks*, Ted Hughes imagines members of his family as different animals. Devising an anthology of 'prefabulous animiles', which might resemble or echo a family member, will be a popular written task to go 'beyond the limit'. The children could use some writing techniques inspired by James Reeves.

# Wings to fly

The reading journeys should have helped your pupils to learn enough about the way Reeves crafted his poems to write themselves with confidence and flair. Refer back to the access strategies and remind them not to settle for the first idea but to search for the best one!

All of the suggestions below need to match style, rhythm and rhyme (if used) to the writing purpose. The best animiles will be variations on known animals but with the addition of distinctive shapes or body forms. Just as the enraged Hippocrump reaches a clumsy end, so your pupils' animile should be involved in something unlikely, funny or unusual!

- Write a poem using one of the names of the 'prefabulous animiles' invented by James Reeves:
  - The Hoverwing
  - The Sniggle
  - The Snyke
  - The Dizz

- Use the same rhythm as Reeves, with an **iambic** foot (unstressed and stressed beat) repeated four times in a line. This gives a regular beat. Invent your own 'prefabulous animile' with an exciting and funny adventure and personality.

- Write a poem which includes the following:
  - A prefabulous animile other than the Hippocrump.
  - A particular setting somewhere else in the valley of the Ump.
  - Other parts of the Purple Lake.

❦ Use the parts of the Hippocrump's body explored in the access strategies to help you plan the content for different stanzas in your poem about a new animile:

- Mouth
- Eyelids
- Humps
- Hair
- Chin
- Claws
- Neck
- Teeth

Those getting stuck may find the structure of the final prompt useful in making a start, but try to leave some space for creativity too. Some of the best English lessons I've known have had a subtle balance of **scaffold with space** (or structure with gaps to provide frameworks and advice) and allowing new ideas to flourish.

Unit 3

# Slowly the Tide Creeps Up the Sand

## 'Slowly' by James Reeves

How successfully can you use repetition in a poem?

# Access strategies

In 'Slowly', James Reeves displays the same kind of ingenious word-play as in 'The Hippocrump' (Unit 2), but it's the repetition which really catches the attention and brings the theme to life for young and old readers alike.

First, ask your pupils what kinds of movements they can think of that are very slow. The first line of Reeves's poem may help: 'Slowly the tide creeps up the sand'.

Ask them to write their answers on a **continuum line** from slow to very slow – for example:

| **Slow** | **Quite slow** | **Very slow** |
|---|---|---|
| Traffic in a jam | Paint drying | Flower growing |

A really good example came up when I was presenting a session to teachers – they said that the first week of the summer holiday goes a lot slower than the last week! Time passing is a fascinating topic. You could extend this activity to include movement. Reeves mentions an old man slowly mounting a stile. What other human activities might involve a slow process?

Next, a **taster draft** should take your pupils' thinking and enthusiasm further. Through discussion with the class, decide on eight slow movements, find pictures on the internet to match each one and then make a visual cycle (like the one on page 35).

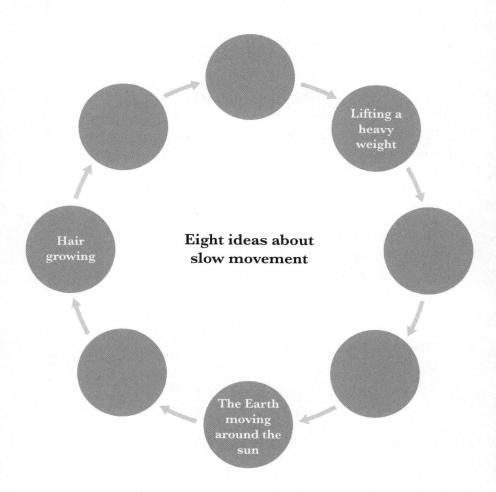

**Eight ideas about slow movement**

Lifting a heavy weight

The Earth moving around the sun

Hair growing

Now the children should try linking the eight slowing moving ideas together in two **stanzas** of four lines each. In the **mini-plenary**, give advice about images, coherence and originality – this will move the learning on for the later application.

# Reading journeys

Your class should be jumping out of their seats now, ready to read Reeves's poem!

**Slowly**

Slowly the tide creeps up the sand,
Slowly the shadows cross the land.
Slowly the cart-horse pulls his mile,
Slowly the old man mounts the stile.

Slowly the hands move round the clock,
Slowly the dew dries on the dock.
Slow is the snail – but slowest of all
The green moss spreads on the old brick wall.

This would be a memorable poem to learn and recite for lots of reasons, but mostly because your pupils will fall in love with it! Pronouncing 'slowly' at the right pace will be critical and will build towards the longer, final line. Don't forget to 'obey' the dash and hesitate – that sets up the **denouement**. Some drama exercises might help the children to learn the poem and understand it. Can they practise the movements of the snail or the carthorse? Could they try symbolising the spread of the moss in movement or mime?

Use the following **radial questions** to support comprehension as appropriate. Why not allow your pupils an element of choice? Here, the analytical question is supported by prompts and direction indicators for any pupils who get stuck. The earlier engagement becomes important because now the brain is working around the words and phrases and placing them into a broader context of prior reading.

*Bob says ...*

*Make sure the questions you use stimulate new concepts that are then discussed in the class. Questions are not just to assess understanding but to prompt further enquiry!*

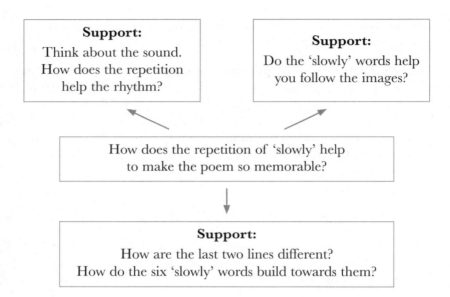

If you set the central question first, you can then be prepared (along with your teaching assistants) to offer support as appropriate. You don't need to split your class into three tables by ability as this can programme their responses. This is a rich resource with an objective that all can share – each pupil can be signposted on their own route to improvement and mastery.

This support strategy can guide your pupils towards accelerated progress based on some 'excellent responses will' success criteria.

**Excellent responses will include**:

❧ As the repetition builds, so does the tension.

❧ Each image resonates and we think about it – the shadows crossing the land stay in the mind.

❧ The dash after 'snail' sets up the final telling image.

❧ The last line lingers and lingers just as time passes – slowly!

❧ The rhythm alters to ignite our responses at the end.

These suggestions should help teachers to deliver the kind of knowledge which can be applied repeatedly through the curriculum; priorities can be selected and explored in simpler language with your class. It's a guide to what you might teach explicitly and as a response to pupils' questions.

*Bob says ...*

*Throughout the book I am including 'excellent responses will' to help deepen your knowledge base so that your class learning dialogue is rich. The technical detail can be shared with your pupils in simple ways, whether in didactic sessions or with **talking partners**. The support questions may be enough to guide their comprehension but you will also need to know the fine detail to **dig deeper** where necessary.*

# Beyond the limit

Compare the effect of the repetition in 'Slowly' with other poems:

- 🍂 'Silver' by Walter de la Mare
- 🍂 'I Remember, I Remember' by Thomas Hood
- 🍂 'Amulet' by Ted Hughes
- 🍂 'Twenty-Six Letters' by James Reeves
- 🍂 'Busy Day' by Michael Rosen

Flood your pupils with reading! They will love finding repetitions in the poetry anthologies in your school library. Why not ask them to select classifications for the poems they discover? Here are some suggestions:

- 🍂 Humour: which repetitions support humour?
- 🍂 Tone change: which repetitions introduce changes of tone?
- 🍂 Assonance: which repetitions repeat clever vowel sounds or **assonances**?
- 🍂 Unsuccessful: which repetitions are unsuccessful, silly or overdone?

Finally, the most able pupils could experience a very different style by comparing 'Slowly' with 'What is Pink?' by Christina Rossetti (Unit 4) or 'I Started Early – Took My Dog' by Emily Dickinson (Unit 15 in *Opening Doors to Quality Writing for Ages 10–13*).

# Wings to fly

The recitation, the access strategies and the drama should have set up openings for the children to write with confidence. Which writing tasks appeal to them?

❦ Use the word 'quickly' or any word implying speed in a poem. Let that be your repetitive word.

❦ Add a new stanza to Reeves's poem.

❦ Follow Reeves's method and use six lines which begin with a repeated word and then make the last two lines different – with an impact!

❦ Write a poem using repetition to help make the final line linger in the imagination.

❦ Use repetition for humour in any clever way.

❦ Keep to the 'slowly' theme but modernise the images to a city environment.

❦ Focus on one image, like the hand moving round the clock. Can you write a poem just about that, featuring repetition as a way of deepening meaning?

❦ The final line is worth some deeper thinking, at least for the more able. The creeping of moss over a wall is imperceptible yet it will change the whole look of the wall eventually. That is very profound. I wonder if some of your pupils could craft some original writing around the image of the wall. What happens to the wall over many centuries? What other things around us are changing that we may not notice? A longer narrative poem with an 'epic' feel is possible here – perhaps inspired by fairy tales.

## Bob says ...

My final 'wings to fly' suggestion is meant to open you up to negotiating with your pupils! Sometimes it is dialogue with the children that can produce the most inspiring and challenging titles, so why not use **areas of potential** like the previous examples and personalise routes to the top as much as you can. Above all, make sure you make the links between learning from James Reeves to applying that learning in fresh ways – that is, from quality text to quality writing!

# Colour Your World

## 'What is Pink?' by Christina Rossetti

Can you take this chance to practise and improve surprise endings in poetry?

## Access strategies

Before reading this beautifully fluent poem by Christina Rossetti, get your class to experiment with colour associations. Make sure more unusual colours or combinations are included. Try a **see, think, wonder** chart to explore how the children feel when a colour is used for a particular place or image.

| Colour | Noun | See | Think | Wonder |
|--------|------|-----|-------|--------|
| Yellow | Sun | A blinding light which I must not look at. | How bright and comforting it is. | How long has it been there? |
| Red | | | | |
| Ultramarine | | | | |

It would be useful to introduce the 'beyond the limit' reading (see page 49) and thinking immediately and browse through some of the colour poems suggested.

*Bob says ...*

*Thinking habits tend to condition learners' approaches, so developing the tendency to go out on the periphery of expectation is essential. Expect unusual colours and you will get unusual answers!*

Offer your pupils the first four lines of Rossetti's poem:

What is pink? A rose is pink
By a fountain's brink.
What is red? A poppy's red
In its barley bed.

The **rhyming couplets** support the flow of the argument and a pattern is set up of question and answer. But the most interesting technique to imitate is the sense of colour contrast – pink against the water, red against brown barley. This strikes the mind's eye with vivid precision!

Can your pupils produce a **taster draft** on the theme of colours? There should be four lines with specific success criteria.

Source II

**Excellent responses will**:

❦ Include rhyming couplets.

❦ Include a rhyme which supports meaning but does not seem forced.

❦ Include a question about a colour.

❦ Emphasise the colour by contrasting it with a different colour background.

Crafting these four lines should stretch the children's minds – and there is so much to be learnt! Use **talking partners** to get them comparing first lines and then put the **evidence spotlight** onto a favourite image within a group. Ask someone in each group to talk about the best expression of a colour from across the taster drafts. This will give you a chance to comment on why they are promising and how they can be developed further.

Your pupils will love reading the full poem with you now. If you wish, ask them to anticipate the images of white, yellow, green and violet that Rossetti will use.

Source 12

### What is Pink?

What is pink? A rose is pink
By the fountain's brink.
What is red? A poppy's red
In its barley bed.
What is blue? The sky is blue
Where the clouds float through.
What is white? A swan is white
Sailing in the light.
What is yellow? Pears are yellow,
Rich and ripe and mellow.
What is green? The grass is green,
With small flowers between.
What is violet? Clouds are violet
In the summer twilight.
What is orange? Why, an orange,
Just an orange!

# Reading journeys

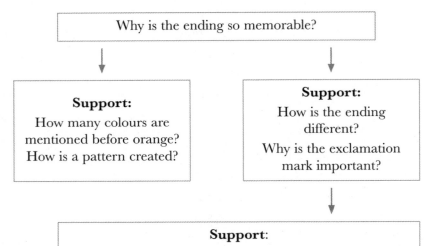

> **Why is the ending so memorable?**

> **Support:**
> How many colours are mentioned before orange?
> How is a pattern created?

> **Support:**
> How is the ending different?
> Why is the exclamation mark important?

> **Support:**
> Draw your favourite images of the items listed in the poem or find pictures on the internet. Cut them out and place them in a line. How is the orange different?

I have tried a different shape here. Rather than the questions radiating outwards, the key or **killer question** is at the top. This will be challenging for all the class. For those who are not yet ready to answer it, I have scaffolded downwards so that easier tasks and prompts can act as signposts. Eventually, many more will master the killer question.

Excellent responses to this evaluative question should include some understanding of the impact of that last couplet on the reader. When I first read it, I was astonished and I laughed quietly too! It seemed so clever. It wasn't a belly laugh – more of an appreciative chuckle. Your pupils should now have some awareness of how, colour by colour, the impressions grow and sometimes the **metre** varies for effect. For example, 'Rich and ripe' has an emphasis on single syllable words which alliterate too. Then, the use of 'orange' as a noun, with the persuasive exclamation mark, brings the poem to a wonderful climax.

### Bob says ...

Young pupils won't be able to express the meaning in the way I have, but they can make early attempts to identify and articulate technique and fall in love with the beauty of the poem. The more knowledge you and your colleagues have about the poem, the more confident you can be about inspiring deeper thinking in all learners.

If the children now learn and recite the poem, it will deepen their understanding and appreciation of it. The kind of repetitive structures that Rossetti uses will make this process a real joy for you and the whole class. It should help them to realise the importance of the waves of colour, which build to a crescendo at the end. Try it at a parents' assembly and I'm sure the parents will love the ending too!

## Beyond the limit

Link in some of these poems to your study of 'What is Pink?' to give your pupils a much broader appreciation of techniques and styles:

❦ 'The Grey Horse' by James Reeves

❧ *How the Animals Got Their Colours: Animal Myths from Around the World* by Michael Rosen

❧ *Sing-Song: A Nursery Rhyme Book* by Christina Rossetti (which includes 'What is Pink?')

❧ 'A Green Cornfield' by Christina Rossetti

For deeper thinking about the repetitive technique in the poem, compare this poem with Unit 3 on 'Slowly' by James Reeves.

Ask any pupils ready for 'beyond the limit' writing to compose an anthology of poems which portray colour in as many ways as they can think of – borrowing Rossetti's 'Rainbow' idea would be good for a title.

**Link reading** should widen understanding so that some of your most able pupils can start to experiment with colours as symbols of moods or emotions. It might be surprising how well they can do!

# Wings to fly

As so often with the reading of rich, quality texts, the multilayered engagement with literary themes can lead quite naturally to the desire to apply ideas in pupils' own writing. To fulfil the challenging objective, set this statement as a standard expectation: 'All poems should feature colours and build towards a final, surprising ending for the reader to enjoy!'

❧ Develop the earlier taster draft into a poem which imitates Christina Rossetti's style but uses different colours and ends differently.

❧ Write a poem with the same colours but different images or associations.

❧ Write a whole poem about the colour white. You can explore different associations of white.

❧ Write a whole poem about the colour red. You can explore different associations of red.

❧ Write about the colours in your home.

❧ Write about the colours of the countryside or a town.

❧ Link colours with a feeling or an emotion – for example, a black day might be a sad one.

❧ Write about your favourite sports team's colours.

If any of the children are stuck, try this structure and ask them to add creative words in the missing lines:

---

### What is Pink?

By _____
What is red? A poppy's red
In _____
What is blue? The sky is blue
Where the clouds float through.
What is white? A swan is white
Sailing _____
What is yellow? Pears are yellow,
Rich and _____
What is green? The grass is green,
With _____
What is violet? Clouds are violet
In _____
What is _____
Just _____

---

A final writing tip comes from Arthur Miller, the famous American playwright, who once said: 'If I see an ending, I can work backward.' If you are ever stuck, try working out the surprise first!

Martha Reaney (Year 2) from Hawley Primary in Hampshire called her poem 'Colours' – she certainly included a clever ending. I hope you and your pupils like it.

### Colours

What is yellow? A daffodil is yellow
Near an ocean scene so mellow.
What is green? A leaf is green
On a windy road so lean.
What is peach? Skin can be peach
And it changes colours on the beach!
What is lavender? Lavender is lavender
Why lavender, just lovely likeable lavender.

Compare it with this poem by Robyn Welsh from Broadstone First School in Poole, who is in Year 1:

### What is white?

What is white? A swan is white.
What is yellow? The sun is yellow.
What is green? The grass is green.
What is brown? THAT bear is brown!

# The Nymph and the Goblin

## 'Overheard on a Saltmarsh' by Harold Monro

Can you learn how to write an unusual poem using dialogue?

### Access strategies

Harold Monro has written many inventive poems which are accessible to young readers. He was the proprietor of the Poetry Bookshop in London during the 1910s and 1920s and supported many other poets of the time. You will also enjoy 'Great City' in *Opening Doors to Famous Poetry and Prose* (Unit 2).

'Overheard on a Saltmarsh' is a poem with a big impact at the end. How do you feel about it? It still appears in many anthologies and there is a fascination about the themes of beauty and possession which are written about in such a fantastical way. The poem has a distinctive appeal which I would recommend you access by providing the key central line first: 'Hush I stole them out of the moon'.

Tell your pupils this is part of a fantasy poem and ask them:

❦ Who or what is using a word like 'hush'?

❦ How could anyone or anything steal something from the moon?

❦ What might you want that is on the moon?

Maximum imagination is called for with the last question! Use a picture of the moon and the **continuum line** below to stretch their thinking.

| **First ideas** | ←————————→ | **Stretching thinking** |
|:---:|:---:|:---:|
| (to be like the man on the moon) | (moonlight) | (the eyes of a crater) |

Sift and sort ideas and ask groups of children to find reasons for choosing their top three. Now link their ideas to the two mythical creatures in the poem (don't show them the full poem yet though):

❦ What is a nymph?

❦ What is a goblin?

Some brief definitions may help. A *nymph* is a spirit of nature from classical mythology. They are usually very beautiful and live in rural settings, in forests or by rivers. A *goblin* is an evil demon, often of short stature. They feature in medieval stories and fairy tales. Think of Gollum's 'precious' in *The Lord of the Rings* – that certainly helped me to understand the goblin's relish for the green glass beads!

Books and films like *The Lord of the Rings* may have helped your pupils' awareness of fantasy creatures like nymphs and goblins, but paintings found on the internet may help too – for example, *A Nymph in the Forest* by Charles Amable-Lenoir. If you use images of famous paintings, you can ask the pupils to write down the typical features of nymphs and goblins on sticky notes which they can then stick onto the images.

Now, look at the illustration on page 54.

Can your pupils suggest themes for the poem they are about to read based on what they see? If you stick copies of the illustration onto the middle of a sheet of sugar paper and create space around it, your pupils can devise plot lines.

Explore potential plots together and make decisions about the best ideas. Good suggestions could go in the middle of concentric circles, with less popular ideas on the periphery.

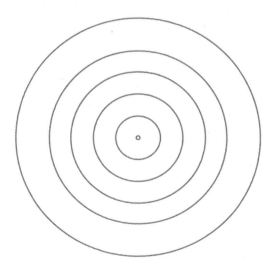

You will get further inspiration from reading these drafts from Year 4 pupils at Hook Junior School in Hampshire.

Once a moon was born from afar,
A special moon born from a star,
With magical powers to hide and seek,
No one could see it, even from a high mountain peak
Hush, I stole them from the moon,
The one that blooms,
The one that zooms,
The one that hides a secret tomb.

*Ava Shackleton*


Trees ripped,
The moon split
　　There was only a cry of pain
　　Coming down the lane
Hush, I stole them from the moon
　　A small voice whispered from behind
A strange spirit loomed
From around the moon
Humming an eerie tune.

*Sophie Culver*

Hush, I stole them
from the moon
    my hand sits
    In pain
    as I carry
    the burning stars away
I stole them from
The blue moon
The dark moon
The forest moon
Hush, I stole them
    from the moon
The burning stars
do not shine
    any more
Hush, I stole them from the moon,
    the moon that has
    been captured
Hush, I stole them from the moon.

**_Owen Smith_**

With some very imaginative teaching (and a slight variation from the poem), the pupils from Hook Junior School have been able to use just one line, 'Hush I stole them out of the moon', to begin to craft some original ideas. At the end of this unit are some more examples of the final poems.

To finish the 'Opening Doors' support, explain what a salt marsh is. Some pictures from the internet will help a lot and here is one definition: salt marshes are coastal wetlands that are flooded with salt water brought in by the tides.

A **taster draft** now will produce the most inventive possibilities – after which your pupils will listen to 'Overheard on a Saltmarsh' with huge interest rather than being baffled! Ask them to write a prose paragraph or **stanzas** from a poem which must include:

❧ A salt marsh setting.

❧ A nymph.

❧ A goblin.

❧ A difference of opinion between the two.

❧ Direct speech from the nymph: 'Hush I stole them out of the moon'.

After the feedback, offer some advice on how to develop the best ideas – the ones showing coherence and originality. Two pupils who read well could now take the parts of the nymph and goblin in a recital.

## Overheard on a Saltmarsh

Nymph, nymph, what are your beads?
Green glass, goblin. Why do you stare at them?
Give them me.
      No.
Give them me. Give them me.
      No.
Then I will howl all night in the reeds,
Lie in the mud and howl for them.

Goblin, why do you love them so?

They are better than stars or water,
Better than voices of winds that sing,
Better than any man's fair daughter,
Your green glass beads on a silver ring.

Hush I stole them out of the moon.

Give me your beads, I desire them.
      No.
I will howl in a deep lagoon
For your green glass beads, I love them so.
Give them me. Give them.
      No.

# Reading journeys

❦ How do you know the goblin is frantic to get the beads?

❦ Why exactly does he want the beads?

❦ What is the effect of a direct conversation in a poem?

❦ Might the nymph and the goblin represent wider ideas?

❦ What does the repetition of 'no' tell us?

❦ The nymph has stolen the beads. Does she feel guilty?

Access for younger pupils may still be an issue, so you could try these support questions:

❦ Which parts of the conversation are most dramatic? Why?

❦ How do you know the goblin wants the beads so much?

❦ Why are the beads so precious?

A personal philosophical journey should help to deepen their engagement:

❦ Have you ever wanted something bright, shiny, beautiful or expensive more than anything in the world?

❦ Are beautiful things like jewellery important?

❦ What is more important: the beauty of an item, the cost of an item or what it means to us?

❦ Is wonderful art and poetry important?

You may well find that these discussions do more than anything to develop comprehension of the themes. 'Overheard on a Saltmarsh' is a poem with simple language but a complex form. As such, it's perfect to explore as long as the theme can be explained and shared. You will find the Society for the Advancement of Philosophical Enquiry and Reflection in Education (Sapere) website helpful for more information on philosophy for children: http://www.sapere.org.uk.

# Beyond the Limit

**Dig deeper** by linking 'Overheard on a Saltmarsh' with other poems featuring conversations:

❧ 'The Fruits, the Vegetables, the Flowers and the Trees' by Carol Ann Duffy

❧ 'Go-Kart' by Michael Rosen

❧ 'Who Are We?' by Benjamin Zephaniah

Other poems by Harold Monro will also broaden and deepen understanding:

❧ 'Goldfish'

❧ 'Milk for the Cat'

❧ 'Great City'

Monro's poems can be found at: http://www.poemhunter.com/harold-monro/.

*Bob says ...*

*You should notice the difference in confidence between pupils with no prior understanding of mythology and those who can reference the words 'goblin' and 'nymph'. This demonstrates that any unseen poem is understood for its style, theme and intention via all the other poems the children have read in the past. Planning for 'beyond the limit' work will help with this process.*

# Wings to fly

The children's sustained writing can now be as inventive as possible. An important question for them to consider is: what is your poem trying to say that is new?

For planning, it would be a good idea to suggest that they devise two characters, a setting and a key phrase.

Monro was writing about the appeal of beauty and using mythical figures with particular associations to express it. Your pupils can imitate the technique and have fun by choosing, with your support, one of the following titles or ideas:

❦ Overheard on a …

❦ Hush, I Stole It from the Stars!

❦ Moon Grabbers! Two other mythical creatures argue in a setting of your choice about a theft from the moon. Invent a new beautiful possession which has been stolen.

❧ How I Stole the Green Glass Beads from the Moon (by Nina Nymph!)

❧ Better Than Voices of Winds That Sing!

❧ What else does the nymph have on the saltmarsh which the goblin wants? Does he succeed on obtaining it?

**Excellent responses will**:

❧ Include a convincing poetic dialogue.

❧ Match the style of speech to the speaker.

❧ Be inventive about questions and answers.

❧ Maintain an appropriate rhythm.

❧ Link the setting with the theme.

It may be that reflecting back on the philosophical debate about 'precious' things may help to make the link between feelings and the form with which to express them. The American poet, Robert Frost said: 'Poetry is when an emotion has found its thought and the thought has found words.'

I hope you like the words from the keen young writers at Hook Junior School. They have certainly found creative ways to express their ideas!

## Inspired by 'Overheard on a Saltmarsh'

*Devil, devil where are the delightful dreams?*
In my staff, Amy. Why do you want them?
*Give them back.*
No.
*Give them back. Give them back.*
No.
*Then I will shout in this palace of dreams,*
*Lie in the moonlight and screech for them.*
Amy, why do you love them so?
*They are better than fairies or mermaids*
*Better than sweet voices that sing*
*Better than any lady's fair hair*
*Nasty dreams on a ring.*
Hush, I stole them from the angels.
*Give me the dreams I want them.*
No.
*I will howl in the lake of memory*
*For my happy dreams, I love them so.*
*Give them me, give me.*
No.

### *Hannah Poulter*

## Inspired by 'Overheard on a Saltmarsh'

Dragon, dragon
I stole you from the forest
Floor.
No, you didn't
Yes, I did
No, you didn't

I can go down there
And ask them.
I can blow that horn
Until every leaf
And every tree
Falls to the floor.
I can ask the whole village
I stole you from the forest floor.

No, you didn't

You are finer than the biggest tree
You are finer
than the world,
finer than
my miniature house,
finer than
any nature.

Dragon, I stole
you from the
forest floor.

*Owen Smith*

# Pictures in My Head

## 'A Child's Thought'
## by Robert Louis Stevenson

How well can you use images which interlink in your writing?

### Access strategies

Your pupils will love fantasy stories and fairy tales, but can you help them craft something fresh where images interlink?

Show them the illustration on page 70 before they see the Robert Louis Stevenson poem. What do they think the poem is going to be about? You could show them the picture on an interactive whiteboard and ask for words or phrases that link with it.

**Zoom in** on one image from the poem, 'Gardens where magic fruits are found', and start a **chart attack** to collect the children's impressions of the garden and the fruit:

| Garden | Fruits |
|---|---|
| How big? | Magic in what way? |
| What shape? | Do the fruits look unusual? |
| How is it landscaped? | |

Ask your pupils to develop their ideas into a stanza all about magic fruit. What title would they give to their stanza or to the illustration? What do your pupils now think the poem they are about to read will include?

Now share the poem with them:

### A Child's Thought

At seven, when I go to bed,
I find such pictures in my head:
Castles with dragons prowling round,
Gardens where magic fruits are found;
Fair ladies prisoned in a tower,

> Or lost in an enchanted bower;[*]
> While gallant horsemen ride by streams
> That border all this land of dreams
> I find, so clearly in my head
> At seven, when I go to bed.

---

Further access strategies could include:

- ❦ What else could dragons prowl around?

- ❦ Use **extra dimension ideas** to stretch the imagination further. How did the bower become enchanted? How did the ladies become imprisoned?

- ❦ Extend the magic fruit idea into writing about new kinds of fantasy fruit. Try a different paragraph for each fruit (with pictures) or a different stanza for each fruit if it's a poem.

A **taster draft** at this point will make the link between the talk for learning and the writing process.

# Reading journeys

To ensure that comprehension skills are being developed and know-ledge deepened, keep the focus on the poem itself now, and make the link between a quality text and quality writing.

How many pupils can try the **hardest question first**?

---

[*] If necessary, explain that 'bower' means the shady place beneath climbing plants in a garden.

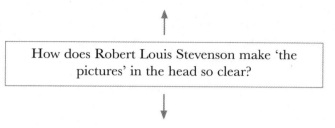

How does Robert Louis Stevenson make 'the pictures' in the head so clear?

Support resources could include:

🐛 What is the special meaning of 'prowling'?

🐛 What is a 'fair' lady?

🐛 How many words or phrases remind us of our favourite fantasy stories?

🐛 Does a word like 'gallant' make us think of any particular story (e.g. King Arthur and the Knights of the Round Table)?

🐛 Could you teach the pupils about **rhyming couplets** and the effect they have in the poem?

🐛 What is a first-person narrator? Does the boy telling us personally about his 'pictures' help us to visualise his thoughts?

# Beyond the limit

Exploit your pupils' engagement to suggest all sorts of **link reading** connected with castles, dragons and fairy tales. To be ambitious, why not explore different images across films and stories. For example, compare the princess in Hans Christian Andersen's *The Snow Queen* (and how it was adapted in the film *Frozen*) with Snow White in *Snow White*, a story by the Brothers Grimm (which was adapted by Walt Disney as *Snow White and the Seven Dwarfs*). This should help to stimulate original images and imaginative twists for writing ideas.

*Bob says …*

*Have you ever wondered why certain pupils write a striking original phrase or try to use an unusual word? I recently read this opening to a narrative by a Year 2 pupil:*

---

'Days rolled into weeks, and weeks into months with no rain …'

---

*It's a long way from 'Once upon a time', isn't it! It will have come partly from what she had read before, partly from talk at home and partly from the overall imaginative stimulus she must have had – but a talented teacher added to that mix too! But it's a complete mystery where it's **really** come from – that's part of the delight!*

When creating original fantasy images, why not use the 'pictures in my head' theme to jump-start thinking about new kinds of dragons, princes and castles? I often see best practice when teachers expect the unexpected and articulate it.

Robert Louis Stevenson was often ill as a child and there are a number of other poems which link with the 'pictures in my head' theme – for example:

❦ 'Bed in Summer'

❦ 'Escape at Bedtime'

❦ 'The Land of Counterpane' (see Unit 4 of *Opening Doors to Famous Poetry and Prose*)

❦ 'The Land of Nod'

❦ 'The Little Land'

❦ 'Young Night Thought'

I would recommend Stevenson's famous collection for children, *A Child's Garden of Verses*, particularly for younger pupils, as it has retained its feel for a child's imagination. A wide selection of Stevenson's poetry can be found at: http://www.poetryloverspage.com/poets/stevenson/stevenson_ind.html. Unfortunately, I've not been able to track down the original publication details for 'A Child's Thought' but it is widely attributed to Robert Louis Stevenson and is included in several modern children's anthologies.

Ask your pupils to go 'beyond the limit' by compiling their own 'Child's Garden of Verses' inspired by Stevenson.

# Wings to fly

Some of these titles and approaches should encourage originality and help to stretch the mind:

1.  New Thoughts in My Head

    Add new phrases to the gaps below and link with images:

    At seven, when I go to bed,

I find ——————————
Castles with ——————
Gardens where —————
Fair ladies ——————————
Or lost in ——————————
While gallant horsemen ——
That border all this————
I find, so clearly in my head
At seven, when I go to bed.

---

**Excellent responses will**:

❧ Demonstrate original images.

❧ Use rhyme to support meaning.

❧ Create new convincing thoughts!

2.  Write a poem or a story about: What Happens to the Gallant Horsemen *or* the Fair Ladies *or* the Prowling Dragon?

A support for writing could be to visualise and draw each episode in planning and turn each one into stanzas or paragraphs. For example, the gallant horsemen might:

❧ Rescue a giant trapped in the sky.

❧ Get a lift in the giant's palm to land on the castle's turret.

❧ Burst into the tower to find the fair ladies turned into stone.

The children could try drawing the episodes in a particular shape to reflect the meaning. For instance, if the plot returns to the beginning at the end they could use a circle:

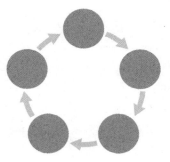

If the story has a dramatic start and images are used to develop the theme in episodes, try:

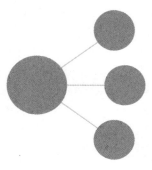

3.  My Stories, My Dreams

    A free choice to write about the stories you love of any kind, and how heroes, heroines, tragedies or romance might crowd into your head at night!

    Excellent responses for questions 2 and 3 would include:

    ❧ New images linked together effectively.

    ❧ Originality.

    ❧ A sense of storytelling.

    ❧ Sensible use of stanzas or paragraphs for sections.

4.  Write a poem entitled 'At Seven, When I Wake Again'. Show how reality replaces the imagination. What happens when you wake up?

# He's Behind You!

## 'The Elf Singing' by William Allingham

Can you experiment with varied styles of writing and suit the style to your theme?

### Access strategies

This wonderfully quirky poem by Irish poet William Allingham is lively and funny but very clever too! Try giving your pupils some opportunities to reflect around names and associations. The following **context thinking** chart might help. It simply gives some prompts for the children to access prior learning from as many areas as possible.

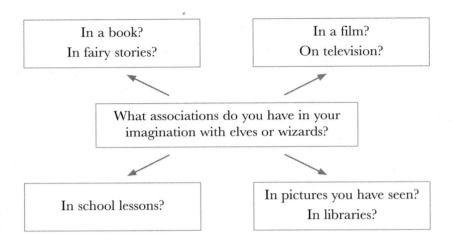

In groups, they could then collate all the associations, words and titles into a shape – perhaps a tree or an exploding volcano of possibilities.

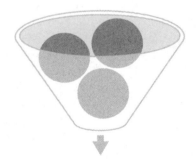

How many associations can each group place in the exploding volcano of possibilities?

Now show your pupils the illustration on page 82:

🐛 Why might the elf be sitting on a twig?

🐛 Tell them that the wizard, who is not in the picture, can change shape. What shapes can they think of?

🐛 Which shapes might help the wizard to join the elf on the twig?

🐛 Ask each group to place their wizard shapes on a **continuum line** with reasons for their favourites at the right end. Here is the start of a continuum line:

Worm          Butterfly          Gorilla          Wizard
                                                  (Reason?)

Ask them to predict the story which will be told in the poem. A **taster draft** could now be written in prose or poetry to deepen engagement and explore creative ideas about the twig, the elf and the wizard.

Encourage your young writers to set up some tension or humour around the scene on the tiny twig, but leave the storytelling until later. It is a chance to create their wizard!

*Bob says ...*

*In the **mini-plenary** feedback session, try asking first for challenges – for example:*

*\* What did you find hard?*

*Which words did you experiment with?*

*Is your idea about the elf and the wizard your best one?*

*What have you learnt so far?*

*Pitch questions high, discover what is hard for them and advise on how to make progress. There will be genuine breakthrough moments with language and style to celebrate too!*

Now use some fun prompts to get your pupils on the edge of their seats:

❦ Who is ready to hear 'The Elf Singing'?

❦ Who can guess the kind of song the elf may sing in this poem?

❦ Will the wizard be good or evil?

Settle them down for a dramatic reading (initially, I suggest, by yourself):

### The Elf Singing

An Elf sat on a twig,
He was not very big,
He sang a little song,
He did not think it wrong;
But he was on a Wizard's ground,
Who hated all sweet sound.

Elf, Elf,
Take care of yourself.
He's coming behind you,
To seize you and bind you
And stifle your song.
The Wizard! The Wizard!
He changes his shape
In crawling along –
An ugly old ape,
A poisonous lizard,
A spotted spider,
A wormy glider
The Wizard! The Wizard!
He's up on the bough

He'll bite through your gizzard,[*]
He's close to you now!

The Elf went on with his song,
It grew more clear and strong;
It lifted him into air,
He floated singing away,
With rainbows in his hair;

While the Wizard-Worm from his creep
Made a sudden leap,
Fell down into a hole,
And, ere his magic word he could say,
Was eaten up by a Mole.

---

# Reading journeys

Map the quality text to quality writing routes with some drama! Your class can be the branches and twigs of the tree whilst chosen pupils take on the different shapes of the wizard. One pupil can be the lone elf and be ready to imitate floating movements, and another pupil can revel in being the greedy mole at the end! There are a lot of movements to practise and there may be scope for an assembly based on the poem.

---

[*] If necessary, explain that a 'gizzard' is part of the stomach in birds and certain other animals.

Drama could be a very effective way of understanding how Allingham changes his style to match the wizard's pursuit in **stanza** two. As the children involve themselves in the drama, you can start to teach explicit points about structure and style. They will be acting out the very changes in mood that you are teaching them about.

Ideally, your pupils will learn so much from the drama that they will answer the question below with confidence and appreciation.

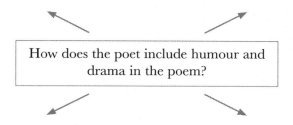

How does the poet include humour and
drama in the poem?

Consider in your more explicit and **didactic teaching** how some of the points below can be covered in depth. This means that **excellent responses will**:

❦ Show how stanza two is longer with a variation from **rhyming couplets**.

❦ Explore how the poet's voice becomes a warning voice in stanza two.

❦ Include the list of shapes which start to get frightening.

❦ Discuss the threat of biting and, in fact, murdering the elf!

❦ Understand the way stanza three shows the power of song and the beauty it represents with words like 'floating', 'lifted' and 'rainbows'.

❦ Explore the unexpected (but fitting) ending with the wizard's shape leading to his downfall.

The most impressive answers of all will show an appreciation of how rhythm and rhyme match the content of each stanza to prompt a reading which elevates the singing elf way above the base motives of the evil wizard. But it may be the success of the drama activities that can bring this to the surface! Now would be a good time to learn and recite the poem too. Pupils may have fallen in love with it by now, so getting some training on how to read it well can only deepen that fondness.

## Beyond the limit

Further mastery could be achieved by encouraging those pupils who are ready to play further with style – for example:

❦ By introducing a third 'mood' – not just contentedness contrasted with threat.

❦ By experimenting with an imperative command in a poem (i.e. the voice of warning: 'Elf, elf, take care of yourself').

❦ By using rhyming couplets in a poem but breaking the pattern for effect.

❦ By experimenting with unexpected endings.

❦ By compiling an anthology of poems.

Linking **wider reading** with learning in lessons will also support attempts to **dig deeper**.

There are other poems by William Allingham to stimulate the mind and provide different examples of his poetry:

❦ 'The Fairies'

❦ 'Robin Redbreast'

❦ 'A Seed'

You can find a compilation of Allingham's poetry at: http://allpoetry. com/William-Allingham.

For a very different image of 'men of magic' from Allingham's wizard:

❦ 'Old Men of Magic' by Dionne Brand

Cross-referencing this unit with Unit 5 on 'Overheard on a Saltmarsh' should also be useful for those pupils who can **dig deeper**.

# Wings to fly

Make the link from the learning points about reading to the application of them in writing. Your budding writers can then compose a poem which has the same clever contrasts in style, mood and pace but which also match the content! There is no need for this to interrupt their natural **flow** but some planning strategies may help:

- Plan four stanzas – like William Allingham.

- Plan the second stanza to be threatening, faster in pace and dramatic.

- Craft an opening which is peaceful and pleasant but still introduces the threat.

- Alternatively, abandon Allingham's stages and invent your own!

Hints for those pupils who need a helping hand might include:

- Start with the evil wizard and work out from there.

- Instead of an elf, a wizard and a twig, use a new setting and develop two different fantasy creatures.

You could offer a choice of titles or keep to 'The Singing Elf':

- The Blade of Grass, the Dew Drop and the Caterpillar

- The Twig, the Branch and the Tree Trunk: A Chorus

- 'He floated singing away, With rainbows in his hair'. Where has the elf gone? What happens to him there?

- The Wizard is a Spider. Write an alternative ending!

- The Song Succeeds. Write a poem where music defeats poison!

Insist on the pupils applying some of what they have learnt from the **reading journey** to stretch their mind and ensure top-class learning. The final outcomes should be worthy of an anthology inspired by William Allingham!

The original interpretation of the children's characters and creatures will be very important. Try asking them to visualise them and/or draw them – they will be bringing their creations to life. Take some advice from Henrik Ibsen, the famous Norwegian playwright: 'Before I write down one word, I have to have the character in my mind through and through. I must penetrate into the last wrinkle of his soul.'

# The Sounds of Silence

## 'Lonely Street'
## by Francisco López Merino

Can you bring silence 'alive' in your writing?

### Access strategies

Work first with the following lines:

where no soul has ever gone by
except that of the wind …

Tell your pupils that this is an image from a poem they will be reading
and appreciating. Can they work out what the setting might be? Can
they locate the 'where' mentioned in these lines? What kind of place
can they think of that might fit the image? Mention that 'no soul' may
mean something more complex than 'no person'.

Sift and sort the range of lonely, deserted or tranquil places the children suggest into **potential for writing categories**. Here is an example using four possible ideas:

❦ Cliff top

❦ Ruined monastery

❦ Empty beach

❦ Shopping centre at dawn

The categories need a further sort based on which option might produce the most originality, challenge and fresh interest for the reader. There is often a tendency for pupils to accept the first idea as the best one, so if this strategy is applied on a regular basis it can help your pupils to think more deeply as a habit. I might decide on a league table of potential like this:

1.  Shopping centre at dawn

2.  Ruined monastery

3.  Cliff top

4.  Empty beach

This is purely a personal choice – but what matters is extending the potential beyond the obvious. I've chosen the shopping centre at dawn because I think it would offer the best opportunity to write about a place that is normally thronging with people in an utterly different way.

To keep it simple with your pupils, you could instead try a **plus, minus, interesting** table.

|  | **Plus** | **Minus** | **Interesting** |
|---|---|---|---|
| Ruined monastery | I'd love the chance to describe crumbling ruins. | Is it a new idea? | It could be spooky. |
|  | I like the fact that it is old. | I've never been to a monastery in ruins! | I need to think of the right story. |

A **taster draft** on a challenging idea should now produce some exciting possibilities. Emphasise a place where the wind can blow through at will. Pictures may help but they might also put too many conventional ideas into the children's heads. The resulting **mini-plenary** and feedback should highlight how successful your writers have been in capturing a deserted or lonely location.

A reading of the full poem by Francisco López Merino, an Argentinian poet writing in the 1920s, could now follow.

---

*Source 21*

### Lonely Street

I love the humble silence of this street
embellished with quiet trees
where no soul has ever gone by
except that of the wind ...

Clouds pause to look at the street
with their heavenly eyes,
and they can tell, by looking at the leaves
whether Fall or Winter have settled their realm.
I love the humble silence of this street
embellished with quiet trees
along which I walked so many Sundays
with my small grove of remembrances ...
When I die, my friend, the best of me
will survive in this street:
the concealed rose of my regrets
and the roaming music of my dreams ...

# Reading journeys

❦ Are your pupils surprised that a street could be the subject of a poem about silence?

❦ Is the street lonely?

❦ Is the poet lonely?

Why not split your pupils into two or three **evidence circles**, with a leader to collect views on these questions and another pupil as a scribe. After ten minutes, scramble the groups, asking one pupil from each group to pick their three best ideas to discuss in another group.

You could use the question below if it helps as an alternative to the three opening questions:

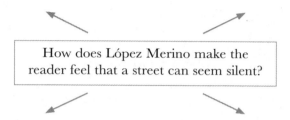

> How does López Merino make the reader feel that a street can seem silent?

Some specific questions may help (or might be raised by the class):

🐾 What does 'embellished' mean?

🐾 Is the figure of speech linked with 'clouds' and 'realm' effective?

🐾 Are the final four lines sad or happy?

🐾 What is the Fall?

If you teach more didactically, you might want to use the enthusiasm engendered to explain why the following points are important in the children's writing.

**Excellent responses will:**

🐾 Mention the personal style – the appeal to the reader as a 'friend'.

🐾 Explain why the line 'embellished with quiet trees' is repeated.

🐾 Suggest why there are capitals for 'Clouds' and 'When'. López Merino appears to start new sections but does not use new **stanzas** thus keeping the street scene coherent and flowing.

❦ Explore the use of **ellipsis**. There is a wonderful echo after 'wind', 'remembrances' and 'dreams' – a kind of resonance of peace and silence.

❦ Explain the two important metaphors at the end: 'the concealed rose of my regrets' and 'the roaming music of my dreams'.

*Bob says …*

*Extended reading supported by deeper knowledge is vital in teaching pupils about poetry. The link can then be made between **new learning** and better writing. 'Lonely Street' provides a lot of scope for advancing comprehension skills, not just 'covering' poetry for the national curriculum. Your talent as a teacher can help to breathe new life into López Merino's words, written almost 100 years ago, to help a new generation produce their own quality writing.*

# Beyond the limit

For the more able, the metaphors at the end certainly deserve more analysis. Can your pupils work out how a 'concealed rose' could symbolise something promising that never flowered or how 'roaming' perfectly captures the wandering nature of idealistic dreams? Could they invent an alternative final couplet with different metaphors?

Your pupils will be inspired by other poems on the sounds of silence theme:

❦ 'Wind' by Dionne Brand

❦ 'For My Son' by Martin Carter

❦ The beginning of 'Preludes' by T. S. Eliot

❦ 'The Road Not Taken' by Robert Frost

❦ 'Great City' by Harold Monro (see Unit 2 of *Opening Doors to Famous Poetry and Prose*)

❦ 'I Wandered Lonely as a Cloud' by William Wordsworth

❦ 'Composed upon Westminster Bridge' by William Wordsworth

This **link reading** will deepen the children's understanding of the theme and add to the variety of styles they might consider in their writing.

# Wings to fly

Can your pupils now apply all they have learnt to create their own 'Sounds of Silence' poem? The title itself emphasises the main challenge and the principal criteria for success: to write about silence in a way that has its own theme, identity and originality. Your pupils' 'sounds' must be imaginative; they can use some of the techniques evaluated in their study of the López Merino poem but in a fresh way. The following pointers may help with the writing process or provide alternative pathways for those who need support:

❦ Describe a street scene in a particular season.

❦ Evoke a silent scene somewhere other than a street.

❦ Keep to a personal style and show a relationship between you, the poet, and your setting and theme. Write in the first person.

❦ Write about your silent street. Is it lonely or peaceful?

And for those who want to **dig deeper**:

- ❦ 'The best of me will survive in this street' – write imaginatively about how this happened (the poet died in 1928).

- ❦ 'The roaming music of my dreams' – write about the dreams still taking shape in the 'humble street'.

- ❦ 'Clouds pause to look at the street' – write about clouds looking down on a different street in a different time.

*Bob says ...*

Take every chance to make a teaching point by referring back to the text itself. A final writing tip might be to emphasise that López Merino has expressed his 'sounds' of silence via his feelings, via nature and via the two beautiful metaphors at the end. There is an irony too in the title since the street is not lonely in spirit at all. Can your pupils reproduce this technique in coherent writing rather than overblown images? That's quite a challenge!

Unit 9

# Pond Dipping

## 'Daddy Fell into the Pond'
## by Alfred Noyes

Can you create a very funny moment in poetry that will make your friends laugh?

## Access strategies

Start opening doors by accessing this objective and text in a variety of ways:

- You could cut up the poem into a strip per line and ask pupils to **sequence** it in groups. This requires a lot of learning about punctuation, line layout and meaning.

- You could offer these lines: ' "Give me the camera, quick, oh quick! | He's crawling out of the duckweed!" Click!' Then ask the pupils to construct a narrative in poetry or prose around these lines. How do they know it's funny? Can they write a **taster draft** on what might happen before and after these lines?

- Give your pupils specific words and phrases, cut up, and then ask them to write a humorous draft using images like:
  - Everyone grumbled.

- 🐾 Dismal day.
- 🐾 Pond.
- 🐾 The gardener slapped his knee.
- 🐾 The ducks all quacked as if they were daft.

🐾 Ask the children to create an **ideas jigsaw**, which is a way of suggesting expected content but leaving a space for other ideas to be interlinked.

Open with a dramatic and funny reading of the whole poem if you judge that no other prior access is needed.

Resource

## Daddy Fell into the Pond

Everyone grumbled. The sky was grey.
We had nothing to do and nothing to say.
We were nearing the end of a dismal day.
And there seemed to be nothing beyond,

> *Then*
>
> *Daddy fell into the pond!*

And everyone's face grew merry and bright,
And Timothy danced for sheer delight.
'Give me the camera, quick, oh quick!
He's crawling out of the duckweed!' Click!

Then the gardener suddenly slapped his knee,
And doubled up, shaking silently,
And the ducks all quacked as if they were daft,
And it sounded as if the old drake laughed.
Oh, there wasn't a thing that didn't respond

> *When*
>
> *Daddy fell into the pond!*

Deepen your pupils' appreciation by asking them to learn and then recite the poem, making the humour 'live' for the reader. The children are going to write in a humorous way later, but it's hard to fully appreciate the effect of a comic poem without reciting it for an audience. It is a good idea to concentrate on some of the verb sounds (e.g. 'quacked', 'laughed') and the alliteration ('dismal day'). The repetition of the lines in italics should bring a lot of audience response!

# Reading journeys

Ask your pupils to invent questions and make comments using **white space thinking** around the text. Make the central issue the parts of the poem that make them laugh and why this is.

Invent your own mark scheme and use it to teach some fresh techniques which will be transferable beyond this objective. It might look something like this.

**Excellent responses will**:

- Show the importance of the italicised exclamations.
- Describe how the rhyming and the **assonance** ('bright'/'delight') lift the mood.
- Mention how the direct speech makes us visualise the sudden hilarity of the moment.
- Explain how and why the reaction from the characters (and from the ducks) makes us laugh.
- Show how the taking of the photograph reminds us how a moment of humour can stay with us.

This is a more open approach, but you may also want to develop comprehension skills by grading your questions along the lines of **Barrett's taxonomy** (see http://www.joebyrne.net/Curriculum/

barrett.pdf). This gives a detailed categorisation of types of comprehension questions which may support a particular methodology. Here are some examples as I've applied them to 'Daddy Fell into the Pond'.

- ❦ Appreciation
  - ❧ Can you find evidence to suggest this poem was written a long time ago?
  - ❧ Why do you think the poet wrote about Daddy falling in, not Mummy?

- ❦ Evaluation
  - ❧ What signs are there that the mood has shifted in the final **stanza**?
  - ❧ Why is the final stanza longer?
  - ❧ How does the rhyme scheme support the meaning?

- ❦ Inference
  - ❧ What mood do the children appear to be in at the start, and how do we know?

- ❦ Reorganisation
  - ❧ Can you explain the main events of the poem in the order in which they happen?

- ❦ Literal
  - ❧ What does 'grumbled' mean?
  - ❧ What is duckweed?

I have presented these suggestions in the reverse order of the norm! This is because by trying the **hardest question first** with some of your pupils, you can plan from the top and distribute easier questions as appropriate. It means differentiation can come quite naturally from pupils working from prior learning to new goals but sharing the same fascinating text.

Many schools with which I work have taken on a different kind of question layout which I call **radial questions** (see the example below). Just imagine using Barrett's taxonomy for your comprehension work but disguising from your pupils any notion of 'easier' or 'harder'. If you select the right question at the right time, you can also get your pupils involved in the process. It's a simple but powerful variation on conventional question setting.

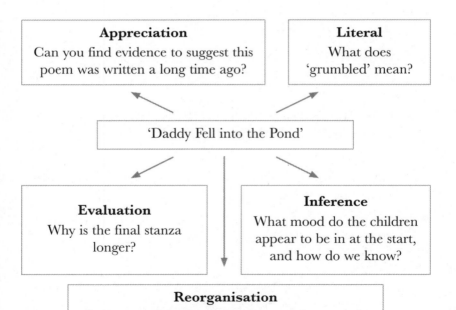

# Beyond the limit

Try including a more investigative question which some of your pupils will be ready for: can you use the internet to find evidence of which type of camera might have been used by the boy in the poem?

This will take your group of detectives on a **discovery path** which will lead to deeper learning about Alfred Noyes, about history and about photography. It's quite a challenge if any of your pupils are up for it! Expect them to get stuck and return to you with questions but solve the problem in the end.

Other **link reading** possibilities could include:

❧ Other Alfred Noyes poems such as 'The Highwayman'
❧ *My Dad Thinks He's Funny* by Katrina Germein (see http://www.booktrust.org.uk/books/children/booklists/222/ for other Book Trust choices about dads)

Poems to deepen our understanding of humour:

❧ 'The Boneyard Rap' by Wes Magee
❧ 'Chocolate Cake' by Michael Rosen
❧ 'The Michael Rosen Rap' by Michael Rosen

Your pupils will absolutely love the raps, which will give them quite a contrast between a traditional poem and modern rhythms!

Try these too for plenty of laughs – but plenty of teaching opportunities too when it comes to technique and style:

❧ 'Please Mrs Butler' by Allan Ahlberg

❦ 'Colonel Fazackerley Butterworth-Toast' by Charles Causley

❦ 'On the Ning Nang Nong' by Spike Milligan

❦ 'Rat It Up' by Adrian Mitchell

## Wings to fly

Now your pupils can apply many of the techniques and ideas they have learnt to their own humorous writing.

Which titles or ideas do they like?

❦ Mummy Fell into the …

❦ Continue 'Daddy Fell into the Pond' using the same style.

❦ Instead of a pond, choose a different setting for a disaster which is funny.

❦ Try writing a poem with the same mood change – from dismal to hilarious.

❦ If you loved the raps, why not try one!

❦ If you enjoyed 'Chocolate Cake', why not write about eating just a bit too much of something else!

If the children get stuck making a start, try these starter lines:

❦ My sister frowned, rain on her brow …

❦ I was grumpy and grey, fed up with play … when …

Or perhaps a few thoughts might help the process:

❦ Will the poem be in a particular style, just like Alfred Noyes's? Could some of your pupils pick the same rhyme scheme and stanza layout?

❦ What methods could you use to make the poem funny?

❦ Which of the titles seem most interesting for writing?

❦ Will you try a stanza-by-stanza plan first?

❦ Will you use italics for effect?

❦ What will be the central event? Will others find it funny?

❦ Will you try a song or rap?

❦ Will you make your poem rhyme? You don't have to! If it does rhyme, it's to help the meaning.

❦ How will your poem sound when it is read out? Remember a poem should have its own rhythm.

This poem from Hetty Dixon (Year 1) at Broadstone First School in Poole will inspire you and your pupils. She decided she liked the first title – getting mummy involved!

### When Mummy Got Stuck in the Ladder

Everyone groaned.
We all felt tired.
We had nothing to say and nothing to play.
Then Mummy got stuck in the ladder!

We laughed so hard, silently and slowly.
We sounded like goats in a field.

Part 2

# Opening doors to prose

Unit 10

# The Making of World-pap

## *The Water Babies: A Fairy Tale for a Land-Baby* by Charles Kingsley

How well can you create an original underwater fantasy?

### Access strategies

Read the opening of the extract from Charles Kingsley's *The Water Babies* and ask for questions and comments around the meaning of 'world-pap'!

Now, as soon as Tom had left Peacepool, he came to the white lap of the great sea-mother, ten thousand fathoms deep; where she makes world-pap all day long, for the steam-giants to knead, and the fire-giants to bake, till it has risen and hardened into mountain-loaves and island-cakes.

World-pap?

Try sounding out Kingsley's hyphenated word – they will love it! Now, ask the children to invent other hyphenated words that could be substituted for 'world-pap' in the passage. In other words, what other image might capture the sense of what is being manufactured? Key questions to support those who need it might be:

❦ What is the 'white lap'? Can you understand this figure of speech?

❦ Who might the 'sea-mother' be?

❦ What are the steam-giants and fire-giants making?

❦ What kind of fantasy world is being described?

Some of your pupils might like to try alliterations like 'fluid-flour' or 'global-gunge'!

Now, a **taster draft** will convert this energy into more sustained writing. Ask for a continuation of the underwater scene.

### Excellent responses will include:

❦ A sense of being under the ocean.

❦ A sense of fantasy and a suggestion of what is in the 'white lap'.

❦ Some kind of sea creature cooking beneath the waves!

Limit your pupils to a description of the scene for now – there is no need to wander into narrative just yet. Let their imaginations capture the wonder of the setting and find words for it. They can develop this later on in some more sustained writing.

In the **mini-plenary**, ask questions like:

❧ What is your sea-kitchen like?

❧ What are you pleased with?

❧ What was hard?

❧ What needs improving?

❧ What is original?

*Bob says ...*

*You will have your own plans for deeper learning but your pupils can suggest ideas too. Play* **reject or accept** *by asking groups to move the best ideas (written on sticky notes) to the middle of a dart board shape with other ideas graded outwards (see also Unit 5). The further from the centre, the less they like the idea. Now they must justify their choices! Which ideas get placed on the bullseye?*

Before reading the longer extract, summarise how your pupils think the plot will develop:

❧ What will happen to Tom?

❧ How will the steam-giants and fire-giants feature?

❧ Is the great sea-mother evil?

In *The Water Babies,* Tom is a chimney sweep who drowns and becomes a water baby and encounters a new world beneath the sea. Written in 1863, it's a moral tale in tune with Victorian times. This extract comes from Chapter 8.

Now, as soon as Tom had left Peacepool, he came to the white lap of the great sea-mother, ten thousand fathoms deep; where she makes world-pap all day long, for the steam-giants to knead, and the fire-giants to bake, till it has risen and hardened into mountain-loaves and island-cakes.

And there Tom was very near being kneaded up in the world-pap, and turned into a fossil water baby; which would have astonished the Geological Society of New Zealand some hundreds of thousands of years hence.

For, as he walked along in the silence of the sea-twilight, on the soft white ocean floor, he was aware of a hissing, and a roaring, and a thumping, and a pumping, as of all the steam-engines in the world at once. And, when he came near, the water grew boiling-hot; not that that hurt him in the least: but it also grew as foul as gruel: and every moment he stumbled over dead shells, and fish, and sharks, and seals, and whales, which had been killed by the hot water.

And at last he came to the great sea-serpent himself, lying dead at the bottom; and as he was too thick to scramble over, Tom had to walk round him three-quarters of a mile and more, which put him out of his path sadly; and, when he had got round, he came to the place called Stop. And there he stopped, and just in time.

For he was on the edge of a vast hole in the bottom of the sea, up which was rushing and roaring clear steam enough to work all the engines in the world at once [...]

# Reading journeys

See how many pupils are confident enough to answer the open question below. If they get stuck, support could take the form of the suggested prompts.

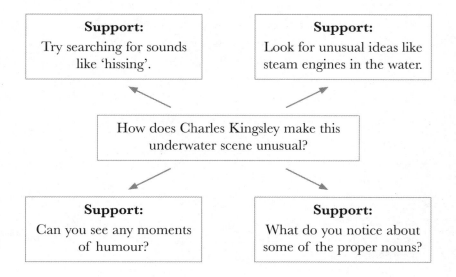

**Support:**
Try searching for sounds like 'hissing'.

**Support:**
Look for unusual ideas like steam engines in the water.

How does Charles Kingsley make this underwater scene unusual?

**Support:**
Can you see any moments of humour?

**Support:**
What do you notice about some of the proper nouns?

Any of the **support scaffolds** can be adapted into easier questions for those pupils needing more practice or help with comprehension issues. The four boxes in this example are deliberately laid out in a radial way to facilitate personalised **reading journeys**, but you can introduce super challenges or new scaffolds according to the needs of your learners.

You might like to share some of the following success criteria with the pupils or use them to inform your own sessions of more **didactic teaching**. Try to evaluate the gaps in the children's knowledge and set new challenges accordingly.

**Excellent responses will**:

- ❦ Show how Tom is portrayed quite naturally as a human under the water − a water baby.

- ❦ Give at least one example of how punctuation influences meaning (e.g. the way semicolons divide sections of the sentence or the way commas mark off clauses).

- ❦ Mention the capital letter for 'Stop' and how this introduces a light-hearted tone.

- ❦ Include writing about the way verbs act repetitively to reveal an engine under the sea.

- ❦ Show how the hyphenated words link unexpected partners (e.g. 'fire-giants' or 'island-cakes').

- ❦ Explain how the cooking, the engine images and the dead creatures give us a mix of impressions, all of which are an unusual spin on fantasy. Is the sea-mother creating mountains and islands like volcanic eruptions?

*Bob says ...*

*Some schools I've worked with are using the 'excellent responses will' statements for CPD for teachers – as a way of deepening knowledge as part of planning routines. The growth in pupils' confidence will soon transmit into top quality classroom discussions on language and meaning.*

# Beyond the limit

You can integrate more practice and **link reading** by planning for rich reading experiences on the underwater theme. A very useful complement to *The Water Babies* extract would be David Wiesner's *Flotsam*. This is a picture book with no text but it provides plenty of challenge with its subtle and sophisticated narrative of a boy who finds an old camera on the beach and gets the film inside it developed! *Flotsam* includes a fantasy underwater episode with superb illustrations, so reading this will enrich the writing possibilities to come. For more see: http://thefishknowthesecret.com/about.html.

Of course, Hans Christian Andersen's *The Little Mermaid* is always popular – there is a good 2014 edition illustrated by Vilhelm Pedersen and Helen Stratton.

Some pupils might be ready for extracts from Jules Verne's *Twenty Thousand Leagues Under the Sea* to stimulate the imagination. This could be linked with non-fiction investigations into the lost civilisation of Atlantis – supposedly destroyed by an earthquake or a tsunami 9,000 years before the Greek philosopher Plato mentioned the event. Did

Atlantis exist? Could a fabulous city still be waiting to be discovered somewhere in the Mediterranean?

Whatever **link reading** you choose, it should enable a much sharper insight into the kind of writing which will fulfil the objective of being original.

## Wings to fly

The reading of quality texts should lead inevitably to quality writing, as long as the access strategies are effective. Ask your pupils to reflect on what has been learnt so far about creating unusual images and stories – for example:

- The steam engine image under the sea.
- The fantasy of a human living under the water as a 'water baby'.
- Wiesner's use of the old camera and the pictures it has taken.
- Kingsley's techniques – some of which are listed in the 'excellent responses will' list on page 116.

Make a coherent link between the learning around the extract, the quality discussions, the taster draft and the choice of prompts below. The quality text is now opening doors to ambitious writing possibilities!

- What is sea-twilight like? Capture the images, colours and sensations of the ocean floor as darkness comes.
- Who else makes world-pap under the sea? Describe them and what they do in detail.

❦ Write a story about the sea-serpent and a water baby.

❦ What happens when Tom comes to a place called 'Go'?

❦ Continue the story in a similar style using fantasy and humour.

You could photocopy and cut up these prompts and then put them in an envelope. Ask your pupils to work on different possibilities for more than one idea before negotiating with you which one has the right level of challenge. Match different planning methods to the pupil.

| Story | Beginning | Middle | End |
|---|---|---|---|
| What happens when Tom comes to a place called 'Go'? | Sees beautiful ruined city. He must go to it. | Setting and adventure. He finds an exotic box. | Reveal the contents of the box. |

*An example of conventional planning*

| Story | Ending | Problems | Original Moments |
|-------|--------|----------|------------------|
| What happens when Tom comes to a place called 'Go'? | 'Go' is a chance to go to the surface – Tom becomes an earth baby. | How do I describe 'Go'? Is it a person, a song, a feeling, a place? | Start with Neptune? 'Go' is actually 'Goafteryourheart'. Can Tom find the heart of a shipwreck or the heart of time? |

*An example of creative planning*

For those pupils ready to do a variation on the creative planning and follow it up with a visual map of their story, there is a much deeper journey available which may produce more originality within the context of more risk. Consciously searching for new ideas will help. The author Gillian Cross has said: 'The older I get, the more my curiosity grows, and every book I write is a new exploration.' So, make sure your pupils write no ordinary undersea tale!

# Master No-book and the Fairy Teach-all

## *Uncle David's Nonsensical Story about Giants and Fairies* by Catherine Sinclair

Can you learn how to adapt a fairy tale in a creative way?

## Access strategies

First try exploring some of these names from Catherine Sinclair's tale – a very early example of a children's story from 1839. Ask the pupils to link each name with a likely personality:

❦ Master No-book

❦ Fairy Do-nothing

❦ Fairy Teach-all

❦ Giant Snap-'em-up

Now, get them to plan a possible plot around a chosen shape. It might be episodes along a **continuum line**:

It might be episodes around a meandering river shape – you could ask the pupils to draw or summarise the main events and descriptive scenes at each 'bend'.

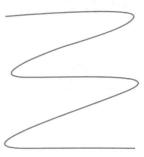

Mountain shapes are popular, giving the opportunity to plan a climax or **denouement** first at the top of the shape:

You could ask them to link their ideas with an unusual setting mentioned in the story, such as Castle Needless:

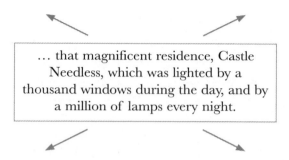

… that magnificent residence, Castle Needless, which was lighted by a thousand windows during the day, and by a million of lamps every night.

Try offering **signposting questions** for those who can go deeper:

🐾 How will you introduce new characters?

🐾 Is there a way of making all the names fit a particular pattern and sound?

🐾 How will you write in a humorous tone?

The last of these questions can be developed into a **taster draft**. Why not ask the children to practise humour, tone and style by crafting a beginning which mentions Master No-book and introduces a story which will be a light-hearted variation on a fairy tale. This could be expressed simply as: Introduce Castle Needless and Master No-book by linking the setting with the person.

Your pupils will now be fascinated by the beginning of the original tale.

### Uncle David's Nonsensical Story about Giants and Fairies

Pie-crust, and pastry-crust, that was the wall;
The windows were made of black-puddings and white,
And slated with pancakes – you ne'er saw the like!

In the days of yore, children were not all such clever, good, sensible people as they are now! Lessons were then considered rather a plague – sugar-plums were still in demand – holidays continued yet in fashion – and toys were not then made to teach mathematics, nor story-books to give instruction in chemistry and navigation. These were very strange times, and there existed at that period, a very idle, greedy, naughty boy, such as we never hear of in the present day. His papa and mama were – no matter who, and he lived – no matter where. His name was Master No-book, and he seemed to think his eyes were made for nothing but to stare out of the windows, and his mouth for no other purpose but to eat. This young gentleman hated lessons like mustard, both of which brought tears into his eyes, and during school-hours he sat gazing at his books, pretending to be busy, while his mind wandered away to wish impatiently for dinner, and to consider where he could get the nicest pies, pastry, ices and jellies, while he smacked his lips at the very thoughts of them.

# Reading journeys

Use this question to help explore the text:

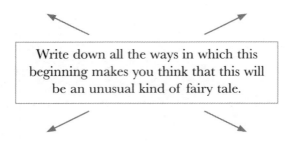

Write down all the ways in which this
beginning makes you think that this will
be an unusual kind of fairy tale.

Support strategies for those who are stuck could be:

❦ Consider the descriptions associated with the boy and, of course, his name. What impression do we get?

❦ What does the description of his eyes and mouth tell the reader?

You could integrate this kind of discussion into the **reading journey**:

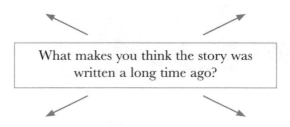

What makes you think the story was
written a long time ago?

A **noticed/noted/not sure** chart might help the children to map their thinking journeys – from impact moments to evaluation.

| Noticed | Noted | Not sure |
|---|---|---|
| 'Mustard' simile | Liked 'tears to his eyes' as it was the lessons as well as the mustard that made him cry. | How could I sum up 'mustard'? I thought it was nice! |
| 'No matter who' | That is his parents! That's strange and he does not live anywhere either. | Does it matter that he has no real home? Is he a real boy? |

For me, it's the wonderful image of the greedy boy that stirs the imagination! If your pupils can understand how Catherine Sinclair creates Master No-book, then it will help them to play with words and devise their own unusual and 'nonsensical' characters.

Further extracts should help with the link between comprehension and creativity:

*Source 29*

### Fairy Do-nothing

The fairy Do-nothing was gorgeously dressed with a wreath of flaming gas round her head, a robe of gold tissue, a necklace of rubies, and a bouquet in her hand of glittering diamonds. Her cheeks were rouged to the very eyes, her teeth were set in gold, and her hair was of a most brilliant purple […]

## Fairy Teach-all

The fairy Teach-all […] was simply dressed in white muslin, with bunches of natural flowers in her light brown hair, and she carried in her hand a few neat small books, which Master No-book looked at with a shudder of aversion.

## Castle Needless

'But in Castle Needless, where I live,' interrupted the fairy Do-nothing, rudely pushing her companion aside, with an angry, contemptuous look, 'we never think of exerting ourselves for anything. You may put your head in your pocket, and your hands in your sides as long as you choose to stay. No one is ever even asked a question, that he may be spared the trouble of answering. We lead the most fashionable life imaginable, for nobody speaks to anybody!'

## Giant Snap-'em-up

If a great mountain had fallen to the earth, it would have seemed like nothing in comparison with the giant Snap-'em-up, who crushed two or three houses to powder beneath him, and upset several fine monuments that were to have made people remembered for ever.

---

You can find the full story of *Uncle David's Nonsensical Story about Giants and Fairies* in *The Oxford Book of Children's Stories* edited by Jan Mark. It is also available online (with an excellent illustration) at: http://www.ubooks.pub/Books/ON/B1/E1119R2838/25MB1119.html.

# Beyond the limit

Try integrating 'beyond the limit' work into your overall expectations – it shouldn't seem like a separate activity. Some of your pupils may wish to explore nonsense poems by Edward Lear (see Unit 1) or the kinds of names used by Lewis Carroll in *Alice's Adventures in Wonderland*. This will deepen their understanding and develop their imagination. They might discover the Jumblies (Lear) whistling and warbling a 'moony song' or the narrator of 'Jabberwocky' (Carroll) with a 'vorpal sword' resting by the 'Tumtum tree'. What kinds of names and phrases might make their writing about Master No-book coherent?

These links should prove useful:

- 'Jabberwocky' (http://www.poetryfoundation.org/poems-and-poets/poems/detail/42916)

- 'The Jumblies' (https://www.poets.org/poetsorg/poem/jumblies)

This unit will give the pupils the opportunity to revisit some fairy tales and explore ideas for adaptations. The following suggestions may help to broaden their reading and lead to clever variations on the traditional storytelling genre:

- *Tales from the Thousand and One Nights* (translated by N. J. Dawood)

- *Grimm Tales: For Young and Old* by Philip Pullman

- *The Happy Prince and Other Stories* by Oscar Wilde

- *The Selfish Giant* by Oscar Wilde

❦ This link gives an overview of tales from across the world: http://fairytalesoftheworld.com/europe/

### Bob says …

Many of us refer to the kinds of 'beyond the limit' thinking and exploring above as **wider reading** or background reading. But I am beginning to ask myself questions about the phrase. It carries with it associations of bolt-on learning, optional routes to achievement or something which could be classed as peripheral. Maybe we need some new terminology, like **link reading**, which encourages teachers to use reading outside school hours as part of the **new learning** within it.

## Wings to fly

Try opening doors to learning with a **routes to quality writing** method. Which routes seem the best for your pupils to write a nonsensical fairy tale?

❦ Develop the ideas from the access strategies and take the planning further using the same names and setting.

❦ Develop the daydreaming idea to write about a naughty boy or girl from years ago who couldn't stop thinking about food! Does it get them into trouble?

❦ Update the food daydreaming idea above to include the kind of food we eat today.

❦ Take up the idea of 'No-book' as a theme. Could it be a funny story of someone who discovers reading?

❦ Put fairy Do-nothing at the centre of the tale. Is a lazy fairy a good subject for a story?

❦ Put fairy Teach-all at the centre of the story. How could this be written in a funny way?

❦ Do you want a super challenge? Try imitating the style of this Victorian writer and give your story a feel of the past with words like 'yore', 'master' for a boy and 'mistress' for a girl.

Try another taster draft to experiment with adaptations and humour: ask the children to write any episode from a chosen route – an opportunity for risk-taking and learning. Your **mini-plenary** can give useful advice on whether the pupils are being original and making everyone laugh too!

*Bob says ...*

*Crafting episodes, possibilities or character profiles can stimulate intense, targeted writing improvement. Explore spellings too and teach grammar – like the importance of understanding prefixes. Then weave all the new learning into the challenge of sustained longer pieces.*

Expect some of your pupils to change routes during this exploration, but encourage them to take responsibility for the choices made and the level of difficulty attempted. You will want to guide them towards an appropriate challenge. The 'wings to fly' writing routes above are a useful starting point, but working through the potential routes first may well stimulate different ideas.

**Excellent responses will**:

❦ Make the class laugh when read out.

❦ Show a clever variation on a typical fairy tale.

❦ Use witty and unusual names in a coherent way.

❦ Include nonsense which is funny but not misplaced.

❦ Conclude in an amusing or moral way using adaptations from traditional fairy tales to make a point.

Unit 12

# Turning the Key

## *The Secret Garden*
## by Frances Hodgson Burnett

Can you build effective tension in your writing?

### Access strategies

*The Secret Garden* is a much loved story and your pupils will enjoy reading this extract and wondering what lies behind the door. Before they do, why not ask them to explore some creative possibilities about gardens which have remained hidden? How can a garden be hidden anyhow? Isn't it too easy to find and enter?

Organise the children into groups and ask each group to devise plans for some secret gardens, and then choose the best one by inventing their own judging criteria. Is the 'best' garden the most fascinating, the most clever, the most unusual or the most mysterious?

The illustration on page 136 should help and these key questions could provide planning prompts:

❦ What will keep the garden secret?

❦ How big is your secret garden?

❦ Is it in a corner of some huge grounds?

❦ Is it a small secluded plot?

❦ Do any unusual plants grow there?

❦ Has a gardener looked after it or has it been neglected?

Each group should choose their best garden – but it must be a secret one!

Now, they need to think about how people can get into the garden, so they can compare their ideas with those in the actual story. Ask them to think of three different ways of gaining access to the garden and then decide which are most creative using a **continuum line**. This could be presented as one class chart with everyone writing their idea on a sticky note and sticking it on the line.

Interesting idea    ←————————→    Unusual, creative, clever idea

Frances Hodgson Burnett uses the idea of a key which opens a concealed door, overgrown with ivy. It would have been quite original at the time (1911) but the idea has endured partly because everything is coherent: Mary, the main character, is an orphan staying with a reclusive uncle; she has been reading about magic; she finds the key buried in the soil; and in the passage she discovers the door under the ivy.

Ask your pupils to write a few sentences as a **taster draft** to experiment with their best idea for entering a secret garden. Use the 'beyond the limit' ideas as appropriate.

For assessment for learning in a **mini-plenary**, try asking:

❦ How original is the draft?

❦ What might need altering?

❦ What is not yet explained?

❦ What has boosted your enthusiasm to continue?

Use impressive drafts to teach the whole class more about coherence, including how spelling, punctuation and grammar can support meaning. Your pupils need to know how English functions as part of a whole, not as a separate exercise.

They should be quite excited to read the extract from Chapter 8 with you, which features Mary finding the door.

---

The robin flew from his swinging spray of ivy on to the top of the wall and he opened his beak and sang a loud, lovely trill, merely to show off. Nothing in the world is quite as adorably lovely as a robin when he shows off – and they are nearly always doing it.

Mary Lennox had heard a great deal about Magic in her Ayah's stories, and she always said that what happened almost at that moment was Magic. One of the nice little gusts of wind rushed down the walk, and it was a stronger one than the rest. It was strong enough to wave the branches of the trees, and it was more than strong enough to sway the trailing sprays of untrimmed ivy hanging from the wall. Mary had stepped close to the robin, and suddenly the gust of wind swung aside some

loose ivy trails, and more suddenly still she jumped toward it and caught it in her hand. This she did because she had seen something under it – a round knob which had been covered by the leaves hanging over it. It was the knob of a door.

She put her hands under the leaves and began to pull and push them aside. Thick as the ivy hung, it nearly all was a loose and swinging curtain, though some had crept over wood and iron. Mary's heart began to thump and her hands to shake a little in her delight and excitement. The robin kept singing and twittering away and tilting his head on one side, as if he were as excited as she was. What was this under her hands which was square and made of iron and which her fingers found a hole in?

It was the lock of the door that had been closed ten years and she put her hand in her pocket, drew out the key and found it fitted the keyhole. She put the key in and turned it. It took two hands to do it, but it did turn.

And then she took a long breath and looked behind her up the long walk to see if anyone was coming. No one ever did come, it seemed, and she took another long breath, because she could not help it, and she held back the swinging curtain of ivy and pushed back the door that opened slowly – slowly.

Then she slipped through it, and shut it behind her, and stood with her back against it, looking about her and breathing quite fast with excitement, and wonder, and delight.

She was standing *inside* the secret garden.

# Reading journeys

Try pitching high with a testing conceptual question and then some scaffolding support.

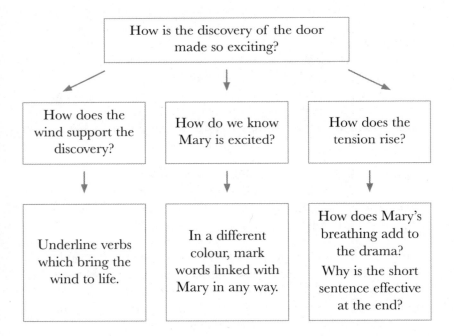

*Bob says ...*

*Use an **inverted question order** if you can make it work. Some pupils will move towards mastery standard by attempting conceptual, higher order questions immediately; others will need the second or third tier of questions to get more basic support.*

In 'Words with Ways: How Grammar Supports Writing' (2015), the author Debra Myhill says:

Teachers with whom I've worked, have developed very effective flexibility to move in second or third tier questions according to need creating a dynamic and personalised classroom; but all the pupils are working with the same content and objective and *going deeper* and deeper as appropriate.

Some schools utilise the **SOLO taxonomy** (Biggs and Collis, 1982; http://pamhook.com/solo-taxonomy) to support the planning of questioning. SOLO stands for the structure of observed learning outcomes. Theoretically, the questions above could be categorised in the following ways:

❦ Unistructural: which words help the reader to learn about Mary?

❦ Multistructural: describe different ways in which the tension rises.

❦ Relational: compare the description of the discovery of the key with the uncovering of the lock.

❦ Extended abstract: Does the tension in *The Secret Garden* remind you of the discovery of something in any other adventure book? How is it similar or different in style?

I would recommend reflecting on Debra Myhill's 'according to need' phrase as it may not be necessary to systematically move all pupils from one tier of SOLO to another. How many of your pupils could move quickly to 'relational' at least?

# Beyond the limit

For younger pupils, some of the following will help with imagining the layout of the garden itself:

❦ *The Curious Garden* by Peter Brown

❦ *Planting a Rainbow* by Lois Ehlert

❦ *Butterflies in the Garden* by Carol Lerner

All pupils will find it useful to look at pictures of large landscaped grounds so they can imagine the secret garden as part of a very large country estate. You could try searching for images online of Blenheim Palace (where there is a secret garden), Hever Castle or National Trust properties in your area.

*Moondial* by Helen Cresswell could deepen the children's thinking as the story is set in a stately home and there is plenty of tension building. Of course, many will want to read *The Secret Garden* itself and Frances Hodgson Burnett's other perennial favourite, *The Little Princess*.

Try extending further with **genre jumping**. Ask the pupils to imagine the extract as a film scene. They could use a simple prompt chart to imagine how each frame might look, supported by a storyboard and freeze frame shots in drama. For example, ask a pupil playing Mary to freeze on how she would look finding the key. Ask the children to comment on what we learn about tension.

| Camera shots, angles and techniques[*] | Effect |
|---|---|
| Long shot | |
| Close-up | |
| Extreme close-up | |
| Medium shot | |
| High angle | |
| Zoom in and out | |
| Editing – how long on each shot | |

There have been a number of film versions of *The Secret Garden*, clips of which can be found on YouTube. However, it might be more interesting to show them the clips after they have completed their own attempt at converting prose into a film script. A useful pattern is **draft/model/explore/improve**, so the 'model' of the film becomes a stimulus rather than an answer.

---

[*] For more information on camera angles and shots see: http://www.skwirk. com/p-c_s-54_u-251_t-647_c-2411/camera-shots-angles-and-movement-lighting-cinematography-and-mise-en-scene/nsw/camera-shots-angles-and-movement-lighting-cinematography-and-mise-en-scene/skills-by-text-type-film/film-overview.

Why not also include a comparison with 'A Garden at Night' (Unit 13 in *Opening Doors to Quality Writing for Ages 10–13*), in which James Reeves shows us how to build tension in a short poem. What do the children think is similar or different about poetry, prose and film?

Are any of your pupils ready to make their own film of their 'Secret Garden'? Have you got a school garden which could be utilised?

## Wings to fly

Some of the tension-building techniques can now be transferred into some original writing! A series of questions should help the process, planned under distinct subtitles:

- Is your garden?
  - Overgrown
  - Undiscovered for years
  - Beautiful but no one goes there

- Does your garden include?
  - Statues
  - Paths
  - Fountains
  - Unusual plants
  - Other features
  - A theme

- Will your story?
  - Be set in the past

- Be set in the present or future
- Be descriptive rather than narrative
- Tell us why the garden is a secret
- Just tell us how the main character gets into the garden

You may wish to add a lot more to this **questionnaire planning** if it helps to build specific ideas the children are developing. They will still need to be converted into a story shape like the river and mountain ones in Unit 11.

If your pupils find it hard to develop and negotiate their own title in this way, then try some of these titles and ideas to help them explore the world of a secret garden:

- Underneath the ivy
- It was not just a secret garden but a secret world!
- The singing plants at midnight in the secret garden
- Storm in the secret garden
- How was the overgrown garden saved?
- Continue Mary's story as she opens the door.
- The robin leads Mary to a secret trapdoor in the garden. What happens?

Remember, excellent responses must show the ability to introduce some kind of tension into the narrative – but there are many ways of doing it!

Unit 13

# The Old Oak Chest

## *The Riddle* by Walter de la Mare

Can you rise to the challenge of writing a tale with a mysterious atmosphere?

## Access strategies

Look at the illustration:

❦ Who or what are the silhouettes?

❦ What kind of meeting is taking place?

❦ Challenge the children to write the first two sentences of a story connected with the illustration.

Now show your pupils this passage from the beginning of *The Riddle* by Walter de la Mare, which was written in 1923:

---

So these seven children, Ann and Matilda, James, William and Henry, Harriet and Dorothea, came to live with their grandmother. The house in which their grandmother had lived since her childhood was built in the time of the Georges […]

When the children were come out of the cab (five sitting inside and two beside the driver), they were shown into their grandmother's presence. They stood in a little black group before the old lady, seated in her bow-window. And she asked them each their names, and repeated each name in her kind, quavering voice. Then to one she gave a work-box, to William a jack-knife, to Dorothea a painted ball; to each a present according to age. And she kissed all her grandchildren to the youngest.

'My dears,' she said, '[…] every morning and every evening you must all come in to see your granny; and bring me smiling faces, that call back to my mind my own son Harry. But all the rest of the day, when school is done, you shall do just as you please, my dears. And there is only one thing, just one, I would have you remember. In the large spare bedroom that looks out on the slate roof there stands in the corner an old oak chest; aye, older than I, my dears, a great deal older; older than my grandmother. Play anywhere else in the house, but not there.'

---

Ask the children to work in groups to collect ideas about objects or toys in an old house.

Encourage each group to find reasons for picking their favourite three objects. They must select objects that will provoke a sense of curiosity in the reader.

| Object from old house | Why might it be mysterious? |
|---|---|
| Worn rocking horse | Who played on it? Why has it been left? |
| Faded painting | Who is the painting of? Why is it there? |
| A scroll with yellowing parchment and something written on it | What is written on the parchment? Why can't anyone pick it up or play near it? |

**Taster drafts** will now hook your pupils into the theme and produce some creative thinking. Why not ask them to set up a mystery, just like Walter de la Mare? They do not need to write a full story yet, but they should start planning their ending (based around their chosen object or old toy) to have a sense of threat – just like the extract. Assess their progress with this in mind and by giving specific advice according to how well they have met the objective. This taster can then link with the 'wings to fly' suggestions for sustained writing on page 150.

*Bob says ...*

*Always get pupils to think about their audience. What will their choice of words mean to a reader? Are they giving readers anything to wonder about? Some pupils I teach at my enrichment centre ask friends quite directly to highlight words or phrases that hint at meaning between the lines.*

# Reading journeys

An **inform and infer** thinking chart will help to deepen the children's understanding of the extract. The idea is to develop the reading skill of accessing hidden meanings as a habit. The habit can then spread to the pupils' own writing, leading to the gradual development of more hidden suggestions and clever innuendo. Here are a couple of examples based around what we learn about the grandmother:

| Inform | Infer |
|---|---|
| She has lived in same house since she was a child. | Grandmother seems very formal. She does not know them. Is she nervous? She has a 'quavering' voice. |
| She has lost her son. | |

Encourage the habit of giving examples as evidence. What do we learn about the children or about the house? A closer reading should reveal how carefully de la Mare picks his words and what this tells us. He leaves doors open in the reader's imagination to fill the spaces with possibility – for example, ask your pupils why the children stand in 'a little black group'.

Spelling development is useful here – ask the children for other examples to link with 'quavering' which have the common 'qu' combination. With all the discussions about the children's grandmother, there is also an opportunity to emphasise that she is 'theirs' – that is, the possessive version of 'their' rather than 'there'. More of your pupils will remember the difference when its importance is emphasised in context!

# Beyond the limit

**Link reading** possibilities can be introduced at any appropriate point in the unit.

Walter de la Mare is an inspiring writer for children and many of his poems have a similar sense of mystery and the unknown as *The Riddle*. The following works would complement and deepen the base from which the children gain writing ideas:

❧ Poetry
- 'The Listeners'
- 'The Magnifying Glass'
- 'Silver'

❧ Short stories
- *The Riddle and Other Stories* (1923)
- *Broomsticks and Other Tales* (1925)
- *The Lord Fish* (1930)

In some ways, the atmosphere of *The Riddle* is reminiscent of stories like *The Lion, the Witch and the Wardrobe* by C. S. Lewis or *The Box of Delights* by John Masefield. Strange oak chests, doorways in the back of wardrobes and magical boxes should help to inspire your pupils' imaginations and link them with stories from their prior reading.

Inspirational picture books include:

- ❦ *The Heart and the Bottle* by Oliver Jeffers
- ❦ *Haunted House* by Jan Pieńkowski
- ❦ *The Arrival* by Shaun Tan
- ❦ *Spooky, Spooky House* by Andrew Wheale

Many of the picture books listed here are very subtle in building reader questioning and inference, sometimes through visual literacy alone. The 'quality text' phrase very much covers sophisticated reading of all types!

## Wings to fly

You can open up more writing possibilities by exploring what happens next in *The Riddle*. Here is another extract indicating more mysterious happenings:

It was evening twilight when Henry went upstairs from the nursery by himself to look at the oak chest. He pressed his fingers into the carved fruit and flowers, and spoke to the dark-smiling heads at the corners; and then, with a glance over his shoulder, he opened the lid and looked in. But the chest concealed no treasure […] The chest was empty, except that it was lined with silk of old-rose, seeming darker in the dusk, and smelling sweet of potpourri. And while Henry was looking in, he heard the softened laughter and the clinking of the cups downstairs in the nursery;

and out at the window he saw the day darkening. These things brought strangely to his memory his mother who in her glimmering white dress used to read to him in the dusk; and he climbed into the chest; and the lid closed gently down over him.

Routes to sustained quality writing could be to:

❦ Continue the story.

❦ Develop an earlier idea from a taster draft using your chosen item, toy or object from an old house that belonged to a relation. Build a sense of mystery.

❦ Include the 'dark smiling heads of the corners' and the 'carved fruit and flowers' in your own story.

❦ Write the story of any one of the other children in the strange old house.

❦ Write the grandmother's story revealing the truth about why they should not play near the oak chest.

❦ Try using one of the suggested items in the following diagram to trigger your imagination and an original mystery.

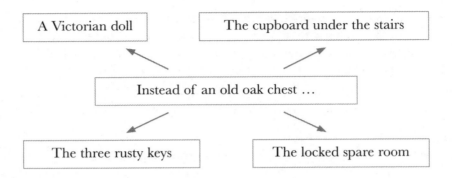

**Excellent responses will** include the ability to infer as well as inform, so the reader asks questions as the narrative develops. The best writing will give some impression of children from the past and include a setting in an ancient old house.

# The Winking Scarecrow

## *The Wizard of Oz*
## by L. Frank Baum

How good are you at creating episodes for a story?

## Access strategies

It can be quite difficult to use very famous stories as a stimulus, but how many of your pupils have actually read Lyman Frank Baum's *The Wizard of Oz* as well as seeing the film? When a narrative is well known there might be a feeling in the room that the lesson will be about something familiar, something popular and therefore something that is great fun! These are powerful, positive emotions to exploit as long as challenge is included too.

Why not start with the illustration:

❦ What does the picture tell us about the Scarecrow's personality?

❦ What evidence do you have for what you say?

❦ Why is he placed high on a pole?

Link your observations with this extract from Chapter 3:

---

While Dorothy was looking earnestly into the queer, painted face of the Scarecrow, she was surprised to see one of the eyes slowly wink at her. She thought she must have been mistaken, at first, for none of the scarecrows in Kansas ever wink; but presently the figure nodded its head to her in a friendly way. Then she climbed down from the fence and walked up to it, while Toto ran around the pole and barked.

'Good day,' said the Scarecrow, in a rather husky voice.

'Did you speak?' asked the girl, in wonder.

---

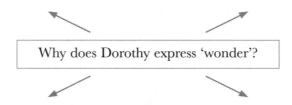

Why does Dorothy express 'wonder'?

Source 36

Your pupils are going to write a new episode for *The Wizard of Oz*, so if they can understand how L. Frank Baum made his scarecrow so memorable, then these lessons can be applied in the 'wings to fly' section.

A **taster draft** can quite quickly build momentum. Try a **javelin** shape to learning where you aim high with minimum fuss and with only a few questions allowed. Make a bridge between the interest in the winking and friendly Scarecrow and a chance to write with invention.

Instead of a scarecrow, ask the children to imagine Dorothy – who is travelling to the Emerald City to find a way back home – has met one of the following:

❦ A farmer without a farmhouse.

❦ A rat without a tail.

❦ A snake that cannot slither.

They should draft a possible introduction of about the same length as the previous extract. The best ones will imply a personality and include something surprising. The children can include some dialogue if they wish. The idea is that the assessment for learning work that follows can signpost improvements and ideas which will support the sustained writing later.

Now, together, read a longer extract (also from Chapter 3) in which L. Frank Baum gives us a detailed visualisation of the Scarecrow. Dorothy has been swept away by a cyclone from Kansas to the land of Oz. Her house crushes the Wicked Witch and she is befriended by the Munchkin people, but to return home she needs help from the

Wizard of Oz in the Emerald City. Her travels along the yellow brick road have begun.

---

Source 37

She bade her friends goodbye, and again started along the road of yellow brick. When she had gone several miles she thought she would stop to rest, and so climbed to the top of the fence beside the road and sat down. There was a great cornfield beyond the fence, and not far away she saw a Scarecrow, placed high on a pole to keep the birds from the ripe corn.

Dorothy leaned her chin upon her hand and gazed thoughtfully at the Scarecrow. Its head was a small sack stuffed with straw, with eyes, nose, and mouth painted on it to represent a face. An old, pointed blue hat, that had belonged to some Munchkin, was perched on this head, and the rest of the figure was a blue suit of clothes, worn and faded, which had also been stuffed with straw. On the feet were some old boots with blue tops, such as every man wore in this country, and the figure was raised above the stalks of corn by means of the pole stuck up its back.

---

The full text is available online at: http://www.gutenberg.org/files/55/55-h/55-h.htm.

# Reading journeys

You will want to choose the right time to show parts of the famous film and explore the way the filmmakers have interpreted this description.

❦ What changes have been made to the Scarecrow and why?

❦ How does L. Frank Baum describe the Scarecrow to help us imagine him in the cornfield?

For those who are stuck, move in with support strategies in the form of prompts:

❦ How is the Scarecrow's head described?

❦ What do you notice about the hat and the suit?

❦ How does the description connect together?

Go 'beyond the limit' for as many pupils as possible with a harder comprehension question:

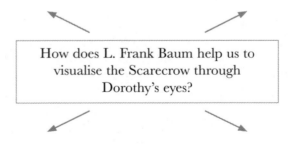

How does L. Frank Baum help us to visualise the Scarecrow through Dorothy's eyes?

**Excellent responses will include**:

- ❦ The story gets its structure from Dorothy's journey and this is one episode.

- ❦ Dorothy sees the Scarecrow 'not far away', so we see him in the same way – almost like a cut in a film moving to a still shot on which we focus.

- ❦ Dorothy's pose, 'gazed thoughtfully', gives us time to turn our attention to the Scarecrow.

# Beyond the limit

**Link reading** could focus on journeys or routes:

- ❦ *Charlie and the Chocolate Factory* by Roald Dahl

- ❦ *The Matchbox Diary* by Paul Fleishmann

- ❦ *Shackleton* by William Grill

- ❦ *The Lion, the Witch and the Wardrobe* by C. S. Lewis

- ❦ *We're Going on a Bear Hunt* by Michael Rosen

- ❦ *Grandfather's Journey* by Allen Say

Both adult and children's literature, old and new, has a deep tradition of voyages or journeys which involve the main character in acquiring knowledge and understanding. The German word *Bildungsroman* is sometimes used in literary criticism to denote a story which tracks some kind of coming of age or journey through life. It's a frequent theme in Victorian novels – Pip in Dickens's *Great Expectations* travels from the world of a blacksmith to that of a rich but sick old lady, Miss Havisham, and then on to London society.

Pupils going beyond the limit may wish to explore different kinds of 'yellow brick roads' of their own making. Ask them to write a sustained story where the main character has to learn about people, situations and themselves through the settings in which they wander. A few of them might turn their tale into a modern day epic!

# Wings to fly

The **reading journeys** should have helped your pupils to explore how episodes can link together to create a unique story. Ask them to return to the taster draft and develop it further with one of these ideas as a possible area for focus:

- Invent three different characters that Dorothy meets on the road to the Emerald City.

- The Scarecrow is made ruler of Oz and is described as 'unusual'. Write about the Scarecrow's journey, learning about being a leader.

- Toto the dog gets lost and follows a red brick road. What happens?

- In the film *The Wizard of Oz*, the actors who play the Scarecrow, the Tin Man and so on also play the farmers back in Kansas. Could you use people from your life and adapt them into characters in your episodes?

**Excellent responses will**:

❦ Create an episode which would fit appropriately into *The Wizard of Oz*.

❦ Successfully imitate L. Frank Baum's style.

❦ Include originality!

❦ Fluently connect one episode to another.

For some pupils, a beginning, middle and end planned on a straight line may be the best way to work, but why should that suit everyone? Other tips for planning their writing could include:

❦ Write down each episode's main points on a sticky note.

❦ Attach the sticky note to a drawing which shows the shape of the story. Some pupils may plan using a mountain showing the climax as a peak; others may show a resolution or **denouement** as a plateau on the top.

❦ Match your planning shape to the story and use the sticky notes for the episodes.

The key questions here will be about coherence:

❦ Do your episodes relate to one another?

❦ How are you linking them?

❦ Do you have your own 'yellow brick road' to give the narrative a kind of glue?

It's now time to write! The questions are over so ask for silence. How easy it is to feel guilty watching your pupils work so hard, and need you less, but your classroom needs to provide an environment for deep concentration. Someone out there could be composing a new children's classic!

### Bob says ...

*Ask your pupils to concentrate – they should get completely absorbed in their imaginations. Everything they have read, seen or talked about is now influencing their minds. Your teaching has provided focus and inspiration!*

The poet Ted Hughes, in *Poetry in the Making,* gives some memorable advice on this process:

---

That one thing is, imagine what you are writing about. See it and live it. Do not think it up laboriously, as if you were doing mental arithmetic. Just look at it, touch it, smell it, listen to it, turn yourself into it. When you do this, the words look after themselves, like magic.

---

# The Psammead

## *Five Children and It* by E. Nesbit

Can you give your fantasy creature an original personality?

## Access strategies

In Edith Nesbit's famous children's story *Five Children and It*, the children are playing in the countryside of Kent, having moved there from London. They are exploring a gravel pit, imagining that it is the seaside, and the hole they begin digging is getting bigger and bigger!

The short extract below from Chapter 1 could start to support access to the theme of creatures discovered unexpectedly:

---

'Suppose the bottom of the hole gave way suddenly,' she said, 'and you tumbled out among the little Australians, all the sand would get in their eyes.'

'Yes,' said Robert; 'and they would hate us, and throw stones at us, and not let us see the kangaroos or opossums or blue-gums or Emu Brand birds or anything.'

Cyril and Anthea knew that Australia was not quite so near as all that, but they agreed to stop using the spades and go on with their hands. This was quite easy, because the sand at the bottom of the hole was very soft and fine and dry, like sea-sand. And there were little shells in it.

---

Ask your class to think about their own experiences based, more likely, on the seaside rather than gravel pits. These key questions could be explored:

- ❦ Have you ever dug very deeply in the sand?
- ❦ What kinds of things might be found?
- ❦ Why is it fun?
- ❦ Did the adults join in?

Now, link personal experiences with the text:

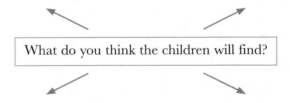

What do you think the children will find?

The final question will deepen the engagement. Mention the title and ask them what the 'it' might be. For some, **white space thinking** with the key ideas marked will support rapid progress; for others, try **scaffolding the space** with some structure – for example:

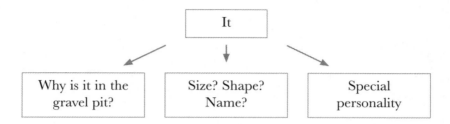

Show your pupils the illustration on page 169. How does their quick and impromptu imagining compare with the picture? What kind of personality do they think 'it' will have?

In your feedback session you should be able to start signposting your pupils towards originality. The best sustained writing at the end will demonstrate how the comprehension of the challenging text has stimulated a higher quality in the writing.

It might be worth linking in the **taster drafts** with the **link reading** possibilities, especially for those who have done particularly well so far. *Stig of the Dump* by Clive King features a creature found in a disused chalk pit full of rubbish. There are some clear similarities! In David Almond's *Skellig*, a half-creature, half-angel is found in a garage and an incredibly imaginative and profound tale develops. In Ted Hughes's *The Iron Man*, the mysterious iron man is the central character from the start – but is he good or evil? By linking with these imaginary creations, your pupils will develop wider evaluative skills by constantly having to compare and contrast across texts.

*Bob says ...*

Link reading and cross-referencing should become a habit, not an exception. **Wider reading** implies a kind of option; link reading is an expectation. All kinds of 'beyond the limit' work should be built in and introduced as early in the process as possible, whereas 'extension' work tends to be bolted on at the end.

## Reading journeys

Now read your pupils some more from *Five Children and It* to reveal what lies beneath the sand. A dramatic reading will pay off. They will be very curious about what is in the hole. Different pupils could speak the different parts.

Anthea went on digging. She always liked to finish a thing when she had once begun it. She felt it would be a disgrace to leave that hole without getting through to Australia.

The cave was disappointing, because there were no shells, and the wrecked ship's anchor turned out to be only the broken end of a pickaxe handle, and the cave party were just making up their minds that the sand makes you thirstier when it is not by the seaside, and someone had suggested going home for lemonade, when Anthea suddenly screamed: 'Cyril! Come here! Oh, come quick! It's alive! It'll get away! Quick!'

They all hurried back.

'It's a rat, I shouldn't wonder,' said Robert. 'Father says they infest old places – and this must be pretty old if the sea was here thousands of years ago.'

'Perhaps it is a snake,' said Jane, shuddering.

'Let's look,' said Cyril, jumping into the hole. 'I'm not afraid of snakes. I like them. If it is a snake I'll tame it, and it will follow me everywhere, and I'll let it sleep round my neck at night.'

'No, you won't,' said Robert firmly. He shared Cyril's bedroom. 'But you may if it's a rat.'

'Oh, don't be silly!' said Anthea; 'it's not a rat, it's *much* bigger. And it's not a snake. It's got feet; I saw them; and fur! No – not the spade. You'll hurt it! Dig with your hands.'

'And let *it* hurt *me* instead! That's so likely, isn't it?' said Cyril, seizing a spade.

'Oh, don't!' said Anthea. 'Squirrel, *don't*. I – it sounds silly, but it said something. It really and truly did.'

'What?'

'It said, "You let me alone."'

But Cyril merely observed that his sister must have gone off her nut, and he and Robert dug with spades while Anthea sat on the edge of the hole, jumping up and down with hotness and anxiety. They dug carefully, and presently everyone could see that there really was something moving in the bottom of the Australian hole.

Then Anthea cried out, '*I'm* not afraid. Let me dig,' and fell on her knees and began to scratch like a dog does when he has suddenly remembered where it was that he buried his bone.

'Oh, I felt fur,' she cried, half laughing and half crying. 'I did indeed! I did!' when suddenly a dry husky voice in the sand made them all jump back, and their hearts jumped nearly as fast as they did.

'Let me alone,' it said. And now everyone heard the voice and looked at the others to see if they had too.

'But we want to see you,' said Robert bravely.

'I wish you'd come out,' said Anthea, also taking courage.

'Oh, well – if that's your wish,' the voice said, and the sand stirred and spun and scattered, and something brown and furry and fat came rolling out into the hole and the sand fell off it, and it sat there yawning and rubbing the ends of its eyes with its hands.

'I believe I must have dropped asleep,' it said, stretching itself.

The children stood round the hole in a ring, looking at the creature they had found. It was worth looking at. Its eyes were on long horns like a snail's eyes, and it could move them in and out like telescopes; it had ears like a bat's ears, and its tubby body was shaped like a spider's and covered with thick soft fur;

its legs and arms were furry too, and it had hands and feet like a monkey's.

Source 40

'What on earth is it?' Jane said. 'Shall we take it home?'

The thing turned its long eyes to look at her, and said: 'Does she always talk nonsense, or is it only the rubbish on her head that makes her silly?'

It looked scornfully at Jane's hat as it spoke.

'She doesn't mean to be silly,' Anthea said gently; 'we none of us do, whatever you may think! Don't be frightened; we don't want to hurt you, you know.'

'Hurt *me*!' it said. '*Me* frightened? Upon my word! Why, you talk as if I were nobody in particular.' All its fur stood out like a cat's when it is going to fight.

---

A **killer question**, one which encourages higher level thinking, and needs a careful reading of the whole text, would help the engagement and comprehension:

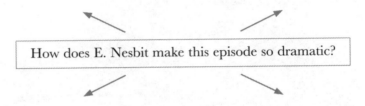

How does E. Nesbit make this episode so dramatic?

The key points learnt here about direct speech, humour, precise descriptions and reader anticipation can all be emphasised in a **mini-plenary**.

Try setting another short **taster draft**:

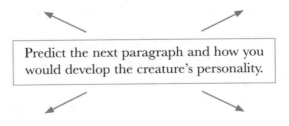

Predict the next paragraph and how you would develop the creature's personality.

Here it is:

---

Source 41

'Well,' said Anthea, still kindly, 'perhaps if we knew who you are in particular we could think of something to say that wouldn't make you cross. Everything we've said so far seems to have. Who are you? And don't get angry! Because really we don't know.'

'You don't know?' it said. 'Well, I knew the world had changed – but – well, really – do you mean to tell me seriously you don't know a Psammead when you see one?'

'A Sammyadd? That's Greek to me.'

'So it is to everyone,' said the creature sharply. 'Well, in plain English, then, a *sand-fairy*. Don't you know a sand-fairy when you see one?'

It looked so grieved and hurt that Jane hastened to say, 'Of course I see you are, now. It's quite plain now one comes to look at you.'

'You came to look at me, several sentences ago,' it said crossly, beginning to curl up again in the sand.

'Oh – don't go away again! Do talk some more,' Robert cried. 'I didn't know you were a sand-fairy, but I knew directly I saw you that you were much the wonderfullest thing I'd ever seen.'

The sand-fairy seemed a shade less disagreeable after this.

'It isn't talking I mind,' it said, 'as long as you're reasonably civil. But I'm not going to make polite conversation for you. If you talk nicely to me, perhaps I'll answer you, and perhaps I won't. Now say something.'

Of course no one could think of anything to say, but at last Robert thought of – 'How long have you lived here?' and he said it at once.

'Oh, ages – several thousand years,' replied the Psammead.

'Tell us all about it. Do.'

---

The Psammead starts to tell its story. The whole text is available at: http://www.gutenberg.org/cache/epub/778/pg778.html, but I want to include one more section here because I'm sure it will inspire much better writing. Give your pupils more of a taste of the originality of the Psammead character to achieve fresh, original writing later. The Psammead tells the children more about its eating habits!

---

'Why, almost everyone had pterodactyl for breakfast in my time! pterodactyls were something like crocodiles and something like birds – I believe they were very good grilled. You see it was like this: of course there were heaps of sand-fairies then, and in the morning early you went out and hunted for them, and when you'd found one it gave you your wish. People used to send their little boys down to the seashore early in the morning before breakfast to get the day's wishes, and very often the eldest boy in the family would be told to wish for a megatherium, ready jointed for cooking. It was as big as an elephant, you see, so there was a good deal of meat on it. And if they wanted fish, the ichthyosaurus was asked for – he was twenty to forty feet long, so there was plenty of him. And for poultry there was the plesiosaurus; there were nice pickings on that too. Then the other children could wish for other things. But when people had dinner-parties it was nearly always megatheriums; and ichthyosaurus, because his fins were a great delicacy and his tail made soup. […]

'it was nearly all sand where I lived, and coal grew on trees, and the periwinkles were as big as tea-trays – you find them now; they're turned into stone. We sand-fairies used to live on the seashore, and the children used to come with their little flint-spades and flint-pails and make castles for us to live in. That's thousands of years ago, but I hear that children still build castles on the sand. It's difficult to break yourself of a habit.'

'But why did you stop living in the castles?' asked Robert.

'It's a sad story,' said the Psammead gloomily. 'It was because they *would* build moats to the castles, and the nasty wet bubbling sea used to come in, and of course as soon as a sand-fairy got wet it caught cold, and generally died. And so there got to be fewer and fewer, and, whenever you found a fairy and had a wish, you used to wish for a megatherium, and eat twice as much as you wanted, because it might be weeks before you got another wish.'

# Beyond the limit

There is quite a literary tradition of children discovering fantasy creatures in unlikely places! There are all sorts of rich reading and ambitious writing possibilities based on further reading of some of these books:

- *Skellig* by David Almond
- *The Iron Man* by Ted Hughes
- *Stig of the Dump* by Clive King
- The 'Nelly the Monster Sitter' series by Kes Gray will stimulate ideas about monsters and settings!
- *The Sand Horse* by Ann Turnbull will delight younger readers – the sand horse wants to join the white horses out in the sea!

Also by E. Nesbit is *The Phoenix and the Carpet*. Ask the children to explore the similarities and differences between the fantasy creatures in the two books. They could also write about any morals they can find in the books they have read. Do they think writers create fantasies to help us understand serious questions, or is it just for fun?

# Wings to fly

The final extract with the memorable breakfast references is important. Your pupils now need to develop their taster drafts into a new creation. These key questions should feed into the planning:

- Why did E. Nesbit use 'Psammead' as a name? What will your name for a sand creature be, and why?

❦ What was detailed and original about the breakfast description? How will your description go beyond what first comes into your head?

❦ Will the Psammead be magical? Will your sand creature grant wishes or is it more a remnant from the prehistoric age?

❦ Will your creature be wonderful, harmful, vulnerable or revengeful? What other feelings might your creature have?

Bear in mind that awareness of your **excellent responses** expectations can sharpen the engagement with the writing possibilities below. After all, if the pupils understand the mark scheme, then it can help them to stretch their minds. So, the following might be helpful to include:

❦ Invent an original and appropriate name.

❦ Show how the sand-fairy's personality is unusual and original.

❦ Show how the children relate to the sand-fairy.

❦ Make the children distinctive and different.

❦ In the longer narratives, include detailed descriptions where relevant.

❦ Make the mood consistent. Is it a humorous or menacing story?

Above all, ask your pupils to consider the reader's reception of their story. Draw them in, like E. Nesbit, to a strange, perhaps amusing, tale and make the central character unique – that is the core objective. Get some inspiration from Stig, the Psammead and the Iron Man, then your pupils can start to find their own writer's 'voice' with something different!

In the Appendix, I've included my own fantasy creature creation in the form of a stone dog. There is nothing quite like teachers and presenters joining in the fun of storytelling!

It's time for the 'wings to fly'! Why not add your own ideas to the ones suggested?

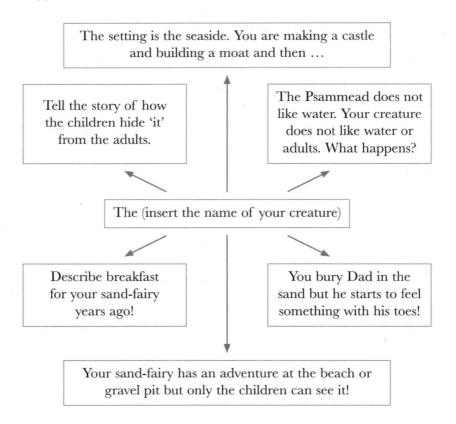

The setting is the seaside. You are making a castle and building a moat and then ...

Tell the story of how the children hide 'it' from the adults.

The Psammead does not like water. Your creature does not like water or adults. What happens?

The (insert the name of your creature)

Describe breakfast for your sand-fairy years ago!

You bury Dad in the sand but he starts to feel something with his toes!

Your sand-fairy has an adventure at the beach or gravel pit but only the children can see it!

# 'The Stone Dog' by Bob Cox

---

Layla was staying at her granddad's for her birthday; but she had been told to go to bed at the third sneeze and the first cough! Her parents were arriving early the next morning. It was always fun spending the night in the old house, alone with her funny and eccentric grandfather.

She tucked herself up under the old-fashioned bedspread with strange floral patterns. She imagined the patterns were a kind of code and she ran her finger along some ancient embroidery. Layla liked the spare room and it was a kind of adventure sleeping there. The rug stretching under the bed smelt musty. Boxes and shelves full of papers filled the wall before her eyes. Yellow scripts flopped over the edge of a partly opened filing cabinet. To the left of her, a half-empty cabinet of matchbox cars clung on to faded wallpaper. Layla liked the collection of ancient road signs, all with warnings about lightning or narrow bridges. They were still part of the matchbox collection but somehow more interesting because they were not actually cars!

Once past the curiosity stage, Layla expected to drop off to sleep but it didn't happen.

Partly, she was annoyed about coming down with a cold, which started to hit like hot needles in the head.

More important though was what was happening outside.

Granddad had a garden office. She had been in it before. It was wooden, painted green and had a large window and a door at the side. Most of the office inside was shelving, photographs and old maps; but it was dominated by a proud, antique desk with random books and papers spread around. Granddad was happy there, sitting in a rocker: writing, painting and thinking.

The office was guarded by a stone dog. Layla loved it as she had always wanted a dog of her own. She could see it out there now, illuminated by a light kept on all night. Its small tail pointed in the air and a lovely, cuddly face seemed to smile at Layla. It was carved in the shape of a small Labrador with eager ears and between its paws a ball lay ready to play with. The stone dog sat in front of the door. No one could get in without passing it.

But Layla could not sleep because the dog seemed different. It was as though he was looking the other way! The head turned back towards the fence, but Layla was sure the head had previously turned towards the neighbours' garden! She knew it was silly but she still could not settle.

She sat up and stared out of the window. The house was quiet but for raindrops on the flat roof above her.

Layla shivered.

A second light came on. This one was set off by a sensor, only lighting up when someone or something came close to the office. Layla gasped.

Who was out there? Who was tampering with granddad's office? Had the stone dog's head really turned round?

Now, through the drizzle and right across the decking of the office came a fox! Slow, orange and padding across the wooden platform, the fox met the dog. Which way was the dog's head turned? Through the drops on the pane it was hard to tell. The wild, crafty and very real fox sniffed the stone ball of the stone dog and looked towards the house.

Then something happened to make Layla start in terror. A third light came on, but this time inside the office!

Layla was losing her mind. Surely, the stone dog was giving her some kind of warning. It was a guard dog after all.

Granddad's room was next door. She crept in and, as always, the grand portrait of a stately home stood over the bed and the photograph of poor grandma – long since dead – still stood on the bedroom table; but the bed was empty! Granddad was gone!

Layla was by herself.

Layla felt desolate, frightened and lost. She had a raincoat hanging up behind the door. She slipped it on, pulling the pink hood over her head. Layla crept downstairs not daring to breathe. She went through the kitchen to the patio door where she had left her shoes. She knew how to open it. Turn the key, lift the lever.

She felt scared staying in the house; she felt terrified of going outside – but she found herself opening the door and stepping out.

She followed the beam of light lingering still on the stone dog and she followed circular stone steps up the garden. The fox still prowled. It seemed as if its bared fangs bent to attack the stone dog but then it turned to Layla. The fox slipped down from the raised decking and faced her. A long, long nose stuck upwards and its mouth opened wide before her! She thought she could see the back of its throat. The teeth showed clear and visible like a saw.

Layla stood in the rain. She was too shocked to move. The fox had slunk away from the lighting sensor and darkness fell again, all except the heavenly beam on the stone dog. She was aware the fox was still there, edging closer in the dark, but somehow seeing the dog made her strong.

She looked towards the eager ears and the cheerful face as if expecting help; and it came! For it seemed to Layla that the dog barked! At least, it was more of a yap than a yelp; but it worked. The fox ran, disturbed, jumping over the neighbours' wire fence.

Layla stared and stared at the stone dog. She felt she should pat him and did so.

But the garden office light came on and the door opened.

'What are you doing? For goodness' sake, come into the dry! You should be in bed!'

Then she was in the office and there was granddad's grey beard and huge form in the middle of the globes and maps and travels of his life. She was being cuddled and warmed and loved.

But the yapping continued. In a basket in the garden office was a puppy, not stone and without the optical illusion of a turning head. A little, shivering golden Labrador leapt into Layla's arms and licked her face and ran all over her coat and wagged its beautiful tail a million times at once! The little puppy even landed a playful bite on Layla's index finger and would not let go! She shrieked with joy!

'It's your secret birthday present and you're not supposed to know until the morning!'

Outside, the stone dog kept guard, oblivious, the stone ball locked between his paws.

---

# Glossary

**Ambiguity**

If something is ambiguous it is open to interpretation. To practise inference and deduction, your pupils need to read more texts with a level of ambiguity. This should then start to inform their own writing ideas.

**Areas of potential**

Rather than setting fixed writing titles, sometimes, by identifying areas of interest, you can help your pupils to develop their own titles. 'Potential' here means that the title stimulates interest but may need further negotiation to find an agreed focus.

**Assonance**

When writers use vowel sounds repeated for effect it is called assonance. Sometimes this is seen in clever rhyming.

**Barrett's taxonomy**

This taxonomy, devised in 1968, provides a categorisation of many types of comprehension questions. See http://www.joebyrne.net/Curriculum/barrett.pdf.

**Chart attack**

There are any number of ways in which pupils can engage with the text by comparing, contrasting, listing or questioning, using simple charts as aids.

**Context thinking**

This is a conscious way of drawing in prior learning, emphasising **link reading** and exploring the map of learning. Instead of support questions set out radially, use questions which ask about context, style and genre. It could even be used as a standard strategy to support more opportunities for synthesising and evaluating.

**Continuum line**

Once you have set two ends of a continuum, the pupils can decide which words or ideas belong at which place along the line. Discourage rapid decision making on 'right' or 'wrong' and instead encourage reflection and the weighing of ideas using evidence. You could say to your pupils, 'To what extent do you think …?' You could first debate a position as a class and then ask the children to stand on a continuum line at the front of the classroom. Explore the issue or idea further and then see who has adjusted their position.

## Denouement

Most stories need some kind of resolution or climax – the denouement – when everything is explained. But writers achieve this in many different ways – often defying convention!

## Didactic teaching

This phrase has been used for a long time to describe traditional teacher instruction. On those occasions when new knowledge needs to be explained or pupils guided very definitely, a didactic method can be employed with success. Outstanding teachers know how to adapt teaching styles and choose the right methodology for the right objective.

## Dig deeper

This phrase has been used most in association with theories of mastery learning, where it is vital to support deeper learning on rich objectives rather than skim the surface and move on quickly.

## Discovery path

Any strategy which encourages choice, debate, options and the taking of responsibility can deepen independence. Paths of discovery rather than a single targeted route can produce quality writing.

## Draft/model/explore/improve

This is a suggested sequence which prevents a model from becoming an 'answer'. One issue with a teacher's model or an explicit example is that pupils can feel that that is what is expected. So, if a **taster draft** is followed by a model which has to be explored and improved, the learning curve should continue to be sharp.

## Ellipsis

Three dots used to show that a word or words have been omitted or are superfluous to meaning.

## Evidence circles

Try turning your classroom into a place where reasons always have to be found for views and opinions. Bring the reasons into an evidence circle for discussion.

## Evidence spotlight

After all sorts of evidence has been collected to answer a rich, conceptual question, put the spotlight on the most convincing reasoning.

## Excellent responses will (include)

This is a suggested way of ensuring that the most ambitious criteria for success are presented up front. It supports classroom discussions about how the most ambitious challenge can be achieved.

## Extra dimension ideas

This is a phrase to help you incorporate the language of challenge into your classroom. Try to make it a habit to include extra dimension possibilities as soon as possible in a unit.

## Flow

Flow is a state of absorbed and energised concentration which was first identified by the Hungarian psychologist Mihaly Csikszentmihalyi. When we are fully immersed in an activity we are said to be in 'flow'.

## Genre jumping

Genre jumping provides many fascinating and challenging possibilities to understand different conventions – for example, comparing a scene from a film with the same event in a novel.

## Hardest question first

This represents a reversal from the traditional linear method of moving from easy to hard. It can be very revealing and surprising, but it must be accompanied by support strategies so that approaches can be personalised according to progress. It is always important to 'plan from the top' to include able learners but there are knock-on benefits for all the class. It does not mean that basic comprehension questions are not needed, but it encourages us to ask questions about when we set them and for whom.

**Iambic**

In poetry, an unstressed followed by a stressed beat is called an iamb.

**Ideas jigsaw**

Cut up and hand out words or phrases from the text to give a feel of the content and genre. The pupils have to use the words in a paragraph or **stanza** but add fresh phrases to complete the jigsaw of ideas.

**Inform and infer**

Develop the habit of sifting out the facts from the meaning between the lines. Explore clear and certain information compared with hidden meanings and suggestions. It is a very helpful access strategy which the pupils can start to apply to any unseen text.

**Inverted question order**

Try harder questions or the **hardest question first** at times to challenge the conventional order of easy to hard. What works for your pupils?

**Javelin**

This is a way of visualising fast, challenging questions or tasks aimed high and with few processes planned.

**Jigsaw**

Initially, each pupil sits in a group which has the same theme to explore – for example, 'characters' in a story. After building ideas on that theme, guided by simple prompt sheets, each pupil moves over to form a new group where the 'character' expertise can be passed on to pupils who have become experts in other areas. This might include settings, beginnings, endings, humour in a story and so on. A jigsaw is formed when the expertise acquired in the first group is linked with the learning from other groups.

**Killer question**

Any question, usually a conceptual one that needs deep exploration, which takes the reader right to the heart of the meaning of a text.

**Link reading**

In your lessons, try cross-referencing books and poems which you expect your pupils to read. This prevents **wider reading** from becoming an optional or a discrete part of the curriculum. Ensure link reading is mapped in as part of continuity and progression.

**Metre**

Metre is a unit of verse which can be used in many different combinations. See http://www.poetryarchive.org/glossary/metre for a brief guide.

**Mini-plenary**

These are feedback sessions with huge opportunities for learning. There should be the chance to share, question and explore progress. You can also teach explicit aspects of spelling, punctuation and grammar in context. Deeper learning and improved outcomes can then follow. Suggested questions might be: What have you found hard? What has interested you the most? How can you improve your writing? What progress have you made?

**New learning**

However obvious it seems, every lesson must include the opportunity for new knowledge and learning – even for the most able pupils in the class.

**Noticed/noted/not sure**

This is a lively thinking sequence to encourage independence, observation and questioning. Pupils have to read any kind of text – visual, media or literary – and respond in three ways:

1. Devise a list of 'noticed' puzzlements in the text.

2. Note down the most important techniques or questions.

3. Include in a third column any other questions.

There should always be words, stylistic points or unusual content which even the most able are not sure about. This will set up your explicit teaching.

**Onomatopoeia**

Onomatopoeic words give expression and life to sounds – for example, the 'rustle' of leaves. Try to get your pupils to use onomatopoeia more in their writing, not just identify it as a figure of speech.

**Philosophy for Children**

See the Sapere website (http://www.sapere.org.uk) for more details on P4C and successful ways to inspire thinking and questioning.

**Plus, minus, interesting**

PMI is a popular **thinking engine** which can support the weighing up of observations and opinions. It's the 'interesting' column which stretches pupils the most, so why not start with that?

**Potential for writing categories**

If you want your pupils to explore writing possibilities, try using planning routes or exploring which titles have the most potential. If this is done quite often, it should support independent thinking and the ability to weigh up the level of difficulty of a title. However, it shouldn't take away those occasions when a pupil knows exactly what they want to do and can't wait to get started!

**Question maze**

Just as there is much trial and error in finding a route out of a maze, so the habit of devising many questions – sometimes in a quite random way – can support deeper thinking.

**Questionnaire planning**

If you want a more detailed way of planning the quality text to quality writing routes, then try a questionnaire where pupils have to make choices under headings like 'setting'. They must complete the questionnaire before starting their story. It is rather like a multiple choice list of questions and it may suit the learning style of some of your pupils.

**Radial questions**

Instead of setting out questions in a traditional linear way, why not offer possibilities for radiating outwards from a central, high level question? This gives you the chance to personalise support and introduce new challenges as appropriate. It is a flexible strategy and encourages the pupils to focus on the quality answers needed.

**Reading journey**

Instead of using the term comprehension why not talk about reading journeys? Emphasise that active and independent approaches to reading make understanding harder texts exciting and full of enquiry – a reading journey for life!

**Reject or accept**

Use concentric circles or a dart board shape to ask your pupils to reject or accept ideas and place the best one on the bullseye!

**Rhyming couplet**

Two lines of verse which rhyme.

**Routes to quality writing**

The 'Opening Doors' strategies work on the basis that there are many different ways to teach English and many different ways in which pupils can fulfil themselves as writers and improve their basic literacy. Pupils take more responsibility for their learning by making informed choices about their planning and titles.

**Scaffold with space** I try to include frames, supports and a clear purpose – but also leave space for the imagination to flow and amazing, unexpected writing to emerge!

**Sequencing**

Sequencing is a popular way of cutting up a text into sections and then asking pupils to reassemble it in the correct order.

**See, think, wonder**

This is a commonly used **thinking engine** where pupils explore what they see first – what it makes them think about in terms of meaning and, more broadly, what kind of wonder the text, visual or resource has stimulated in their imagination.

**Signposting questions**

All kinds of vital prompts can signpost deeper learning opportunities and create an ethos of enquiry in the classroom. Questions which simply persist in making the learner go deeper might include, 'Can you explain fully?' or 'Is there a better answer?' Socratic questioning can help here. See: http://changingminds.org/techniques/questioning/socratic_questions.htm.

**SOLO taxonomy**

The structure of observed learning outcomes (SOLO) taxonomy is widely used in schools, particularly to support mastery learning. Devised by John Biggs and Kevin Collis, it supports the development of understanding through a unit of learning. For more information visit: http://www.learningandteaching.info/learning/solo.htm.

**Stanza**

A stanza is a verse of poetry.

**Support scaffolds**

Planning from the top is essential but this means that support scaffolds are essential too, otherwise some challenges may be too hard. Scaffolds can be pictures, extra questions, a shorter or different text or a modelled idea. Feeding an answer is not the same as a scaffold.

**Talking partners**

A common way of sharing but also improving ideas is to discuss drafts with a talking partner. I recommend varying talking partners throughout a term.

**Taster draft**

The access strategies should include an early chance to write. This kind of draft should be enriching, not laborious. Your young writers can experiment with style and get advice from you at the point of the most intense enjoyment and learning. The taster draft is a powerful learning vehicle for the improved full version they will write later on.

**Think, pair, share**

A popular **thinking engine** where all pupils reflect in silence on a challenging question, then share their thoughts with a **talking partner**. In this way, participation can be expected from all in a whole-class debate.

**Thinking engine**

A generic phrase used to sum up the many ways in which the level of thinking can be developed in a classroom. However, the starting point is having something challenging and interesting to apply the thinking to!

**White space thinking**

This is a very common but effective strategy for encouraging pupils to write notes and questions in the spaces around texts, rather than being limited to answers in boxes.

## Wider reading

The traditional phrase for reading on the periphery of your subject. I advise using the term **link reading** in order to raise expectations and support cross-referencing in lessons.

## Wings to fly

The phrase, 'Wings to fly, not drills to kill', comes from a wonderful course evaluation by a teacher about how her pupils could benefit from more open and creative approaches. Risk-taking lies at the heart of any possibility for pupils to fly. They will do what we expect, so we should signify that writing in unusual ways is exciting. Of course, some will still need formats and templates as support resources.

## Word mosaic

The technique of describing different parts of a whole (e.g. sections of a painting, parts of a creature) and then bringing them together in a word mosaic. The children should explore how the parts contribute to the whole.

## Zoom in

Using the language of media studies can be very useful. Just as a camera zooms in, so too can a teacher offer a magnified view of a particular image or concept by focusing on one part of the text. A visualiser can provide a quite literal 'zoom in' on the subject.

# Bibliography

## Primary sources

Ahlberg, Allan (1984). 'Please Mrs Butler', in *Please Mrs Butler*. London: Puffin.

Allingham, William (2012 [1887]). 'The Elf Singing', in Allie Esiri and Rachel Kelly (eds), *If: A Treasury of Poems for Almost Every Possibility*. Edinburgh: Canongate.

Almond, David (1998). *Skellig*. London: Hodder Children's Books.

Andersen, Hans Christian (2014 [1836]). *The Little Mermaid*, tr. Henry H. B. Paull, ill. Vilhelm Pedersen and Helen Stratton. N.p.: Hythloday Press.

Baum, L. Frank (1993 [1900]). *The Wizard of Oz*. Ware: Wordsworth Classics.

Brand, Dionne (1990 [1979]). 'Old Men of Magic', in Grace Nichols (ed.), *Poetry Jump-Up: A Collection of Black Poetry*. London: Puffin.

Brand, Dionne (1990 [1988]). 'Wind', in Grace Nichols (ed.), *Poetry Jump-Up: A Collection of Black Poetry*. London: Puffin.

Brown, Peter (2009). *The Curious Garden*. New York: Little, Brown.

Carroll, Lewis (2003 [1865]). *Alice's Adventures in Wonderland*. London: Penguin.

Carter, Martin (1990 [1988]). 'For My Son', in Grace Nichols (ed.), *Poetry Jump-Up: A Collection of Black Poetry*. London: Puffin.

Causley, Charles (1979 [1970]).'Mr Pennycomequick', in *Figgie Hobbin: Poems for Children*. London: Puffin.

Causley, Charles (1979). 'Colonel Fazackerley Butterworth-Toast', in Kaye Webb (ed.), *I Like This Poem*. Harmondsworth: Puffin.

Cresswell, Helen (2015). *Moondial*. London: Faber and Faber.

Dahl, Roald (1967). *Charlie and the Chocolate Factory*. London: Puffin.

Davidson, George (ed.) (2015). *Favourite Poems*. London: Arcturus Publishing.

Dawood, N. J. (ed./tr.) (1973). *Tales from the Thousand and One Nights*. London: Penguin.

de la Mare, Walter (1925). *Broomsticks and Other Tales*. New York: Alfred A. Knopf.

de la Mare, Walter (1930). *The Lord Fish*. London: Faber and Faber.

de la Mare, Walter (1941). 'The Magnifying Glass', in *Bells and Grass: A Book of Rhymes*. London: Faber and Faber.

de la Mare, Walter (1979 [1912]). 'The Listeners', in *Walter de la Mare: Collected Poems*. London: Faber and Faber.

de la Mare, Walter (1989 [1920]). 'Silver', in *Collected Rhymes and Verses*. London: Faber and Faber.

de la Mare, Walter (1993 [1923]). *The Riddle*, in Jan Mark (ed.), *The Oxford Book of*

*Children's Stories*. Oxford: Oxford University Press.

Dickens, Charles (2004 [1861]). *Great Expectations*. London: Penguin.

Duffy, Carol Ann (2007). 'The Fruits, the Vegetables, the Flowers and the Trees', in *The Hat*. London: Faber and Faber.

Ehlert, Lois (2003). *Planting a Rainbow*. San Diego, CA: Red Wagon Books.

Eliot, T. S. (2011 [1917]). 'Preludes', in *The Complete Poems and Plays of T. S. Eliot*. London: Faber and Faber.

Fleishmann, Paul (2013). *The Matchbox Diary*. Somerville, MA: Candlewick Press.

Foster, John (ed.) (2002). *My First Oxford Book of Nonsense Poems*. Oxford: Oxford University Press.

Foster, John (ed.) (2010). *I've Got a Poem for You: Poems to Perform*. Oxford: Oxford University Press.

Frost, Robert (2012 [1916]). 'The Road Not Taken', in *A Treasury of Poems for Almost Every Possibility*. Edinburgh: Canongate Books.

Germein, Katrina (2013) *My Dad Thinks He's Funny*, ill. Tom Jellett. Somerville, MA: Candlewick Press.

Gervais, Ricky (2005). *Flanimals*. London: Faber and Faber.

Grill, William (2014). *Shackleton*. London: Flying Eye Books.

Hodgson Burnett, Frances (2007 [1911]). *The Secret Garden*. Oxford: Oxford Children's Classics.

Hodgson Burnett, Frances (2014 [1905]). *The Little Princess*. London: Puffin.

Hood, Thomas (2013 [1826]). 'I Remember, I Remember', in Roger

McGough (ed.), *Poetry Please*. London: Faber and Faber.

Hughes, Ted (2005 [1968]). *The Iron Man*. London: Faber and Faber.

Hughes, Ted (2005 [1970]). 'Amulet' in *Collected Poems for Children*. London: Faber and Faber.

Hughes, Ted (2012). *Meet My Folks*. Faber and Faber.

Jeffers, Oliver (2010). *The Heart and the Bottle*. London: HarperCollins.

King, Clive (2014 [1963]). *Stig of the Dump*. London: Puffin.

Kingsley, Charles (1994 [1863]). *The Water Babies*. Ware: Wordsworth Editions.

Lear, Edward (1980 [1877]). 'The New Vestments', in *The Courtship of the Yonghy-Bonghy-Bo and The New Vestments*. London: Ash & Grant.

Lear, Edward (2012 [1871]). *The Owl and the Pussycat and Other Nonsense*, ill. Robert Ingpen. Dorking: Templar Publishing.

Lerner, Carol (2002). *Butterflies in the Garden*. London: HarperCollins.

Lewis, C. S. (2009 [1950]). *The Lion, the Witch and the Wardrobe*. London: HarperCollins.

López Merino, Francisco (1979 [c.1922]). 'Lonely Street', in Kate Webb (ed.), *I Like This Poem*. London: Puffin.

Magee, Wes (2000). 'The Boneyard Rap', in *The Boneyard Rap and Other Poems*, ill. Keith Brumpton. Hove: Wayland.

Masefield, John (1935). *The Box of Delights*. London: Heinemann.

Milligan, Spike (1973).'On the Ning Nang Nong', in *Silly Verse for Kids*. London: Puffin.

Mitchell, Adrian (2013). 'Rat it Up', in *101 Poems for Children Chosen by Carol Ann Duffy: A Laureate's Choice*. London: Macmillan.

Monro, Harold (1933 [c.1913]). 'Overheard on a Saltmarsh', in *Collected Poems of Harold Monro*. London: Gerald Duckworth.

Monro, Harold (1933[1915]). 'Great City', in *Collected Poems of Harold Monro*. London: Gerald Duckworth.

Monro, Harold (1933 [1915]). 'Milk for the Cat', in *Collected Poems of Harold Monro*. London: Gerald Duckworth.

Monro, Harold (1933 [1922]). 'Goldfish', in *Collected Poems of Harold Monro*. London: Gerald Duckworth.

Nesbit, E. (1999 [1902]). *Five Children and It*. Ware: Wordsworth Editions.

Nesbit, E. (2007 [1904]). *The Phoenix and the Carpet*. Fairfield, IA: 1st World Library/ Literary Society.

Nichols, Grace (1988). 'Sea Timeless Song', in *Come on into My Tropical Garden*. London: A and C Black.

Noyes, Alfred (1979 [1952]). 'Daddy Fell into the Pond', in Kate Webb (ed.), *I Like This Poem*. London: Puffin.

Noyes, Alfred (2014 [1913]). 'The Highwayman', in *Collected Poems of Alfred Noyes: Volume 1*. London: Read Books.

Pieńkowski, Jan (2005 [1979]). *Haunted House*. London: Walker Books.

Philip, Pullman (2013). *Grimm Tales: For Young and Old*. London: Penguin.

Reeves, James (1957). *Prefabulous Animiles*. London: William Heinemann.

Reeves, James (1975). *More Prefabulous Animiles*. London: William Heinemann.

Reeves, James (2009 [1950]). 'Slowly', in *Complete Poems for Children*. London: Faber and Faber.

Reeves, James (2009 [1950]). 'The Grey Horse', in *Complete Poems for Children*. London: Faber and Faber.

Reeves, James (2009 [1950]). 'Waiting', in *Complete Poems for Children*. London: Faber and Faber.

Reeves, James (2009 [1957]). 'The Hippocrump', in *Complete Poems for Children*. London: Faber and Faber.

Reeves, James (2009 [1961]). 'The Twenty-Six Letters', in *Complete Poems for Children*. London: Faber and Faber.

Rosen, Michael (1981). 'Busy Day', in *You Tell Me: Poems by Roger McGough and Michael Rosen*. London: Puffin.

Rosen, Michael (1985).'Chocolate Cake', in *Quick, Let's Get Out of Here*. London: Puffin.

Rosen, Michael (1992). *How the Animals Got Their Colours: Animal Myths from Around the World*. San Diego, CA: Harcourt Brace Jovanovich.

Rosen, Michael (1993). *We're Going on a Bear Hunt*. London: Walker Books.

Rossetti, Christina (2001 [1875]) 'A Green Cornfield', in *Christina Rossetti: The Complete Poems*. London: Penguin Classics.

Rossetti, Christina (2003 [1872]). *Sing-Song: A Nursery Rhyme Book*. Mineola, NY: Dover Children's Classics.

Rossetti, Christina (2012 [1872]). 'What is Pink?', in *Jabberwocky and Other Poems*. Thaxted: Miles Kelly.

Say, Allen (2014). *Grandfather's Journey*. Boston, MA: Houghton Mifflin Harcourt.

Sinclair, Catherine (1993 [1839]). 'Uncle David's Nonsensical Story about Giants and Fairies', in Jan Mark (ed.), *The Oxford Book of Children's Stories*. Oxford: Oxford University Press.

Stevenson, Robert Louis (1885). *A Child's Garden of Verses*. Chicago, IL: M.A. Donohue & Co.

Stevenson, Robert Louis (1996 [c.1885]). *The Children's Classic Poetry Collection*, Nicola Baxter (ed.). Leicester: Armadillo Books.

Strachey, Sir Edward (1868). *Morte D'Arthur* (Globe Edition). London: Macmillan.

Tan, Shaun (2014). *The Arrival*. London: Hodder Children's Books.

Tolkien, J. R. R. (2007 [1954–1955]). *The Lord of the Rings*. London: HarperCollins.

Tolkien, J. R. R. (2013 [1937]). *The Hobbit*. London: HarperCollins.

Turnbull, Ann (1989). *The Sand Horse*. London: Andersen Press.

Verne, Jules (1992 [1870]). *Twenty Thousand Leagues Under the Sea*. Ware: Wordsworth Editions.

Wheale, Andrew (2011). *Spooky, Spooky House*. London: Picture Corgi.

Wiesner, David (2006). *Flotsam*. New York: Houghton Mifflin Harcourt.

Wilde, Oscar (1998 [1888]). *The Selfish Giant*. New York: G. P. Putnam's Sons.

Wilde, Oscar (2015 [1888]). *The Happy Prince and Other Stories*. London: William Collins.

Wordsworth, William (1995 [1807]). 'Composed upon Westminster Bridge', in *Collected Poems of William Wordsworth*. Ware: Wordsworth Poetry Library.

Wordsworth, William (1995 [1807]). 'I Wandered Lonely as a Cloud', in *Collected Poems of William Wordsworth*. Ware: Wordsworth Poetry Library.

Zephaniah, Benjamin. (2000). 'Who Are We?', in *Wicked World!* London: Puffin.

## Secondary sources

Alexander, Robin (2008). *Towards Dialogic Teaching: Rethinking Classroom Talk*, 4th edn. Cambridge: Dialogos.

Clymer, Theodore (1968). 'What is "Reading"? Some Current Concepts', in Helen M. Robinson (ed.), *Innovation and Change in Reading Instruction*. Sixty-Seventh Yearbook of the National Society for the Study of Education. Chicago, IL: University of Chicago Press, pp. 17–23.

Biggs, John and Collis, Kevin (1982). *Evaluating the Quality of Learning: SOLO Taxonomy*. New York: Academic Press.

Claxton, Guy (2002). *Building Learning Power*. Bristol: TLO Ltd.

Dean, Geoff (2008). *English for Gifted and Talented Students: 11–18 Years*. London: Sage.

Eyre, Deborah (2016). 'Beyond Gifted', *National Education Trust* (12 February). Available at: http://www.nationaleducationtrust.net/ShapingIdeasShapingLives238.php.

Forster, E. M. (2005 [1927]). *Aspects of the Novel*. London: Penguin.

Goodwin, Prue (ed.) (2004). *Literacy Through Creativity*. London: David Fulton.